Scorched
Earth

Scorched Earth

Legacies Of Chemical Warfare In Vietnam

FRED A. WILCOX

Photographs by Brendan B. Wilcox

7

Seven Stories Press

NEW YORK

A Seven Stories Press First Edition

Seven Stories Press
140 Watts Street
New York, NY 10013
www.sevenstories.com

College professors may order examination copies of Seven Stories Press titles for a free six-month trial period. To order, visit http://www.sevenstories.com/textbook or send a fax on school letterhead to (212) 226-1411.

Book design by Jon Gilbert

Library of Congress Cataloging-in-Publication Data

Wilcox, Fred.
 Scorched earth : legacies of chemical warfare in Vietnam / Fred A. Wilcox ; photographs by Brendan B. Wilcox. -- A Seven Stories Press 1st ed.
     p. cm.
 Includes bibliographical references.
 ISBN 978-1-60980-138-0 (hardcover)
  1. Agent Orange--Health aspects--Vietnam. 2. Agent Orange--Environmental aspects--Vietnam. 3. Chemical warfare--Health aspects--Vietnam. 4. Chemical warfare--Environmental aspects--Vietnam. 5. Vietnam War, 1961-1975--Chemical warfare. I. Title.
 RA1242.T44W55 2011
 615.9'513709597--dc23

                                            2011023208

Printed in the United States

9 8 7 6 5 4 3 2 1

CONTENTS

Appendices

Introduction

*In the abominable history of war, with the sole exception of
nuclear weapons, never has such an inhuman fate ever
before been reserved for the survivors.*

—Dr. Ton That Tung, Vietnamese research scientist

On April 30, 1975, North Vietnamese tanks smashed into the
grounds of the presidential palace in Saigon. Vietnam lay in
ruins, its towns and cities bombed to rubble, the countryside
seeded with unexploded mines, cluster bombs, and artillery
shells. A decade of chemical warfare had reduced majestic
triple canopy jungles to toxic graveyards. Mangrove forests,
habitats for songbirds and vital to coastal ecosystems, had
turned into eerie moonscapes.

Agent Orange, the most widely used herbicide in Vietnam,
was named after the orange stripe painted around the fifty-
five-gallon barrels in which it was stored. It was a fifty-fifty
combination of 2,4-D and 2,4,5-T, two commercial herbicides
used widely in the United States. The 2,4,5-T in Agent Orange
was contaminated with TCDD-dioxin, a carcinogenic, fetus-
deforming, and quite possibly mutagenic chemical. Nearly
forty years after the last spray mission, scientists continue to
find high levels of dioxin in the food and water near abandoned military bases and in the blood, fatty tissue, and

mother's milk of the Vietnamese who live near these installations.

Making their way through dense jungles, US soldiers heard a cacophony of squawking birds, chattering monkeys, and insects buzzing like high-voltage wires. But after C-123 cargo planes swooped low over the trees, inundating them with Agent Orange, the ground was littered with decaying jungle birds and paralyzed and dying monkeys. Clusters of dead fish shimmered like buttons on the surface of slow-moving streams. "It was," said one combat veteran with whom I spoke, "like walking through a graveyard."

Years later, veterans would recall being soaked like the trees when aircraft jettisoned their herbicides. They'd also remember feeling dizzy, bleeding from the nose and mouth, and suffering from debilitating skin rashes and violent headaches after being exposed to Agent Orange.

Vietnamese caught in the path of herbicide missions complained that they felt faint, bled from the nose and mouth, vomited, suffered from numbness in their hands and feet, and experienced migraine-like headaches. They said that farm animals grew weak, got sick, and even died after being exposed to defoliants. As the use of herbicides escalated, Saigon newspapers risked publishing stories about babies born with heads shaped like mice, pigs, and sheep, about two-headed babies. Peasants whose families had lived on the same land for generations said they'd never encountered such strange phenomena. Doctors and nurses who delivered these babies could not recall having seen similar birth defects before the American War.

Scorched Earth is about a tragedy that, unlike earthquakes, tsunamis, floods, and wars of limited duration, has been maiming and killing people for decades. It is about the aftermath of a chemical warfare campaign that destroyed the lives of several million Vietnamese adults and children. No one can be sure when, if ever, this calamity will end.

In 1983, Random House published *Waiting for an Army to Die: The Tragedy of Agent Orange*, the first book to chronicle the effects of Agent Orange on Vietnam veterans. I'd spent two years interviewing scientists, doctors, lawyers, and young veterans who were sick and dying from diseases that normally do not attack young men. Many of these illnesses were remarkably similar to those from which laboratory animals suffer when they are exposed to TCDD-dioxin. Moreover, veterans from Australia, South Korea, and New Zealand who'd been exposed to Agent Orange were experiencing illnesses—cancer, numbness in their arms and legs, diabetes, and heart problems—similar to those from which US veterans were suffering.

For the next thirty years, I kept track of research on the effects of Agent Orange/dioxin on human beings and animals, taught college-level courses on the Vietnam War, wrote extensively about the war, and worked with veterans to persuade the government they'd served to treat them with dignity and respect, and to compensate them for the long list of illnesses they'd contracted due to their exposure to toxic chemicals in Vietnam.

I have long believed that the missing link that will prove once and for all that Agent Orange destroys human beings would be found in Vietnam. In July 2009, after many long years of preparing to research and write about this link, I flew with my son on the first leg of an arduous investigative journey. On a previous trip to Vietnam, I visited a small base camp that Vietcong soldiers had constructed deep inside of the jungle. Decades after the US Air Force sprayed the area with Agent Orange, this hideaway could easily be spotted from the air. There were no birds and no animals except crocodiles and monkeys with large lumps growing on their skinny bodies. No sign that the jungle would ever return.

My methodology in writing *Scorched Earth* was scientifically anecdotal, or anecdotally scientific. I did not set out to gather mountains of statistics or studies jam-packed with incomprehensible charts and graphs. Instead, I wanted to meet Vietnamese people who'd been exposed to Agent Orange; I wanted to listen to their stories and to hear if their accounts were similar to those of American veterans, as well as veterans from the other nations that sent troops to fight in Southeast Asia. Additionally, I hoped to talk with Vietnamese scientists, doctors, community activists, and others who'd dedicated their lives to researching the effects of Agent Orange/dioxin on human beings. In short, I set out to listen to Vietnam.

I wanted to observe what life is like for impoverished victims of chemical warfare in Vietnam and to record what ordinary Vietnamese have to say about the effects of Agent Orange/dioxin on their families, and how they view their future. In many respects, I was determined to be a kind of medium for people who, as I found, struggle to survive not only their serious illnesses, but the sorrow of knowing that their plight, their destiny, is irrevocable. Their children will never attend school; they will never be able to work, marry, or bear children of their own.

In the opening pages of this book, I give readers an overview of the massive environmental damage caused by the use of herbicides, Rome Plows, and other methods to destroy Vietnam's forests. Proponents of the defoliation campaign told those who challenged the attack on Vietnam's environment that the trees would soon grow back. And while some of the mangrove forests have returned, forty years after the last spray mission wild "American grass" still grows where jungles once stood. Scientists do not know when, if ever, these jungles will return.

In Ho Chi Minh City, I interviewed the doctor who delivered the first headless baby in a Saigon hospital in 1967, and who spent the next forty years researching the effects of dioxin on pregnant women. Late one afternoon, my son Brendan and I were escorted into a locked chamber of horrors down the hall from the children's ward in Tu Du Hospital. Inside this room, monsters float in large formaldehyde-filled glass jars. "Skeptics," said the doctor who accompanied us there, "are more than welcome to visit this room, after which I will be happy to answer their questions."

I set out in *Scorched Earth* to *show* what happens to human beings who are exposed over long periods to TCDD-dioxin, the most toxic small molecule known to science. Researchers who've spent years studying the effects of dioxin on laboratory animals know that pregnant mice given minute doses of this chemical develop cancer and give birth to horribly deformed offspring. They know for certain that dioxin is fetotoxic in pregnant laboratory animals and that it is a human carcinogen. They know that it might well prove to be mutagenic in human beings.

One chapter of this book is devoted to the Vietnam veterans' 1984 class action lawsuit filed against Dow Chemical and other wartime manufacturers of Agent Orange. I also examine the Vietnamese lawsuit, filed in 2004, charging these chemical companies with war crimes. Lawyers representing the plaintiffs in these cases had hoped that the American judicial system would provide a forum for the victims of chemical warfare, one that would grant them redress for their injuries.

This did not happen.

My goal is to introduce readers to the catastrophe we

euphemistically refer to as "the Agent Orange issue." I wish to expand the dialogue and debate over the repercussions of chemical warfare. Vietnam veterans are dying at a rapid rate, and most of them will not live to see—should this ever happen—the chemical companies concede that they manufactured and sold Agent Orange to the military, fully aware that this defoliant was contaminated with TCDD-dioxin and fully cognizant of a process by which the dioxin levels in herbicides might have been greatly reduced.

The war in Vietnam was not the first time that a nation resorted to a scorched earth strategy against an enemy in war; however, it was the first time in human history that, in the process of trying to defeat an adversary, a government inadvertently poisoned its own army, then waited for this army to die.

Vietnam has fought many long and brutal wars against foreign invaders. Its people have survived famine and starvation; they've endured prison, torture, massacres, and mass executions. Now, they are enduring the aftermath of a chemical holocaust.

In the last chapter, readers will find letters that victims of chemical warfare have written to Ken Herrmann, a decorated Vietnam veteran, college professor, director of a college-level study abroad program in Vietnam, and a long-time advocate for victims of Agent Orange.

In these letters, the Vietnamese parents of seriously deformed children, ex-soldiers, and the terminally ill express their grief, their sorrow, and their sincere hope that someone will care enough to help them. They also express their fear that the United States of America may have forgotten about them altogether.

"We, the AO victims," writes one man, "really appreciate your concern for us. The war has been over for almost 30 years. The Americans have begun to forget about us while millions of the Vietnamese people are still living with its disastrous effects. . . . There are many families that are affected into the third generation. We still have no idea when AO will stop affecting the health and safety of my innocent people. It may affect the fourth and fifth generations. The list may be longer."

A widow whose child suffers from serious birth defects writes that she has been spiritually devastated by "knowing that my only child is in danger. As a widow, I don't know what to do to help my daughter. It is most miserable to know that the poisonous water I drank when I was young is the cause of her disease. The poison has passed from my genes to hers."

The United States has yet to send teams of epidemiologists to Vietnam to study the effects of toxic chemicals on the Vietnamese people, and US courts have failed to find ways to hold corporations that care more about profits than people responsible for their actions. Historians will write the final verdict on government stonewalling, political chicanery, and scientific fraud in the long, sad saga of Agent Orange.

Scorched Earth is about a monumental tragedy, but it is also about courage, resilience, determination, love, and what appears to be a remarkable optimism in the face of insurmountable odds.

In Hanoi, we met Phung Tuu Boi, a forester who exemplifies the indomitable spirit of the Vietnamese people. While the war still raged, he began planting trees in defoliated zones. Asked if he wasn't afraid that he might step on a mine or an unexploded cluster bomb, he shrugged and laughed. He has organized teams to plant hundreds of thousands of trees, and he intends to plant millions more.

Dr. Professor Nguyen Trong Nhan, a veteran of the war against France and a prominent Agent Orange activist, insisted that one day the US government and the chemical companies will agree to pay compensation to Agent Orange victims.

"Remember," he smiled, "we Vietnamese have lost many battles, but we always win the war."

Dr. Nhan was not gloating, just expressing an ancient culture's infinite patience and unlimited capacity to endure hardship.

Vietnam is a beautiful, vibrant nation whose citizens are determined to rebuild their country so their children can live in prosperity and peace. All they ask is that the United States government and the corporations that profited from chemical warfare in Vietnam acknowledge the harm they caused and agree to help desperately poor victims of Agent Orange. Until then, they will continue their efforts to show the world the ravages of chemical warfare.

There must never be another tragedy like the one that began in the White House with the momentous decision to launch chemical warfare in a far-off nation that lacked either the ability or the desire to harm the United States of America.

During two research trips to Vietnam, I promised the Vietnamese, who so graciously shared their time—translating for hours on end, arranging transportation to and from interviews, answering a thousand questions—that I would write and publish a book on the legacies of chemical warfare in Vietnam. *Scorched Earth* fulfills that promise.

CHAPTER 1

Ecocide

The destruction brought about by indiscriminate bombing and by the large-scale use of bulldozers and herbicides is an outrage that is sometimes referred to as "ecocide."

—Swedish Prime Minister Olof Palme, United Nations Conference on the Human Environment, 1972

LATE NOVEMBER, 1961, WASHINGTON, DC

President John F. Kennedy is worried. The Vietcong, a pejorative term for those who are fighting against Ngo Dinh Diem's regime in Saigon, are taking over large swaths of the countryside. American military advisors have failed to turn Diem's inept and apathetic troops into a hard-charging army. Vietnam is an impossible terrain, cut to pieces by rivers and canals, covered with dense jungles and snake-infested swamps, populated by man-eating tigers. The enemy knows every inch of this forbidding landscape. Defeating them will require bold new strategies.

And so the president's inner circle discusses the pros and cons of using herbicides in Southeast Asia. It seems that the British used chemicals with some success when fighting guerrillas in Malaysia, and the advisors feel it might be worth testing—and possibly using—chemical defoliants in Vietnam.

Countries like Sweden might complain that the US is violating some international treaty or other, but the regime in Saigon is doing its best to defeat communist guerrillas and needs greater support, the State Department and the Department of Defense support the use of herbicides, and Congress will undoubtedly go along with any program that helps prevent a communist takeover of Southeast Asia.

Secretary of State Dean Rusk assures President Kennedy that "successful plant-killing ops in [Vietnam], carefully coordinated with and incidental to larger ops, can be substantial assistance in the control and defeat of the [Vietcong] . . . the use of defoliant does not violate any rule of international law concerning the conduct of herbicidal warfare and is an accepted tactic of war."[1]

President Kennedy approves the joint recommendation of the State Department and Department of Defense to "initiate a large scale herbicidal/chemical warfare program. Both departments advanced the use of herbicides for defoliation only, apparently recognizing that the destruction of enemy crops was a clear violation of international law and a war crime, and were therefore unwilling to explicitly endorse such a program."[2]

Influential State Department officials such as Roger Hilsman and W. Averell Harriman oppose the use of herbicides in Vietnam, warning that if civilians are harmed, the US might be perceived as a "barbaric imperialist."[3]

Test runs demonstrate that herbicides are highly effective. No more hiding for the Vietcong. Herbicides will drive them into the open, where they will be obliterated. As the war escalates, the military expands the defoliation campaign, spraying enemy supply routes, footpaths, the Demilitarized Zone, the Mekong Delta, and the perimeters of US military bases.

By 1965, 45 percent of the total spraying is directed at crops. If the military suspects that the Vietcong are taking food from a particular area, those fields are completely destroyed. Fields used exclusively by civilians are also doused with herbicides, and in 1967 alone the military uses 20 million liters of herbicides—85 percent to kill forests and 15 percent to destroy crops.[4]

President Kennedy does not live to see the full-scale use of chemical warfare in Vietnam, and historians can only speculate as to whether he would have supported a campaign that clearly violated international laws such as the Genocide Convention, laws that forbid wanton attacks on civilians in times of war.

During the first year of the defoliation campaign, the White House has to approve all targets. Then, in 1962, the South Vietnamese government agrees to assume ownership of herbicides once they are delivered: a clever way of making it appear that the Diem regime, not the United States, is really responsible for and directing chemical warfare in Vietnam.

In 1963, journalist Richard Dudman publishes a series of articles in the *St. Louis Post-Dispatch* and other newspapers, calling the use of herbicides in Vietnam "dirty-war tactics." He writes that the military is not only using herbicides to kill trees, but to poison rice fields. After reading Dunham's articles, Wisconsin Congressman Robert W. Kastenmeier writes to President Kennedy, calling herbicides chemical weapons, and urging him to end the defoliation campaign.

In 1964, a *Washington Post* story describes the "accidental spraying of a friendly village in southern Vietnam which destroyed the rice and pineapple upon which people depended for their livelihood." The next day, editorializing that herbicides pose a risk to Vietnam's civilians, the *Post* calls for an end to the defoliation program.[5]

Commander of the US Air Force General Curtis LeMay

wants to "bomb Vietnam back to the Stone Age." Other people in and out of the government suggest turning the country into a parking lot.

By 1971, the US Air Force has run 19,905 spray missions, an average of thirty-four daily, over the forests, jungles, and fields of southern Vietnam.[6]

The defoliation campaign burns a 5 million acre parking lot, an area the size of Massachusetts, into Vietnam's countryside.

Three administrations—Kennedy, Johnson, and Nixon—continue the defoliation program. Attempts by congressmen like Gaylord Nelson (D-WI) and Charles Goodell (R-NY) to cut off funding for the use of herbicides in Vietnam fail by wide margins. From July 1966 to July 1973, Congress votes one hundred times for appropriations to continue the war in Vietnam, and never votes to curtail or prohibit spending for the herbicide program.[7]

In their pioneering work on the devastating effects of herbicides in Vietnam, Orville Schell and Barry Weisberg conclude that the United States sprayed thirty-seven of Vietnam's forty-four provinces with Agent Orange during the first two months of 1969,

> contaminating 285,000 people, with death resulting in 500 cases. In these raids, more than 905,000 hectares of rice, orchards and other crops were destroyed. Between late 1961 and October 1969, Vietnamese estimate that 43 percent of the arable land and 44 percent of South Vietnam's tropical forests were sprayed at least once and in many cases two or three times with herbicides. Over 1,293,000 people were directly contaminated. Besides forest and mountain areas, large populated areas in the Mekong Delta have been

sprayed as well, including the outskirts of Saigon itself.[8]

In some regions, defoliation changes the amount of rainfall, heat, and wind on the forest floor. Grasses, shrubs, and bamboo spread over the defoliated forests. Bamboo grows into high thickets, preventing hardwood forests from regrowing. Attempts to defoliate, burn, and cut bamboo do little to keep it in check. Vietnamese report that chemicals entering the Mekong River upstream are killing biological life in the estuary. Herbicides are destroying the food wild animals depend on for their survival. Species such as the Javan rhinoceros, elephant, gibbon, and crocodile are in danger.

The destruction of Vietnam's environment is so great that even before the war ends, some scientists are calling it "ecocide."[9]

Operation Pink Rose, a "secret confidential" report from May 1967, confirms that herbicides were not only used to destroy Vietnam's jungles and mangrove forests, but also to kill off row crops, particularly rice. Made public information in 1988, the report states that the "VC/NVA troops located in areas where crop defoliants have been used are often faced with a food crisis. *The defoliant is nondiscriminate* [sic] *and it makes little difference whether the enemy produces its own food or relies on procurement from the local population.*"[10]

Rural Vietnamese hate and fear herbicides, prompting US psychological warfare teams to shower the countryside with cartoon leaflets that show a bewildered peasant talking with a confident South Vietnamese government official.

MR. NAM (frightened peasant): "The Viet Cong say: 'The Republic of Viet Nam army sprays on your farm a terrible poison to kill you.'"

GOVERNMENT OFFICIAL: "The Viet Cong hide in bushes, robbing and killing people who travel on buses and trains. This is why the government sprays the foliage, so that the VC can't terrorize citizens like Mr. Nam."

MR. NAM: "But how about my crops? Are these sprays harmful to people, our animals, the soil or our drinking water?"

OFFICIAL: "Look at me. You see how healthy I am. Everyday, while performing my duties, I usually breathe in a lot of the spray. Look at me, do I appear sick to you?"

MR. NAM: (Greatly relieved) "I now resolve never to listen to Viet Cong propaganda."

OFFICIAL: "Mr. Nam and all others understand the real reasons behind the Viet Cong's false propaganda about the defoliant spray."[11]

According to Operation Pink Rose:

The defoliant is usually 100 percent effective in the destruction of row crops and consequently the VC/NVA are denied such crops when they are sprayed. The only exceptions noted are certain tuberous plants such as potatoes and carrots . . . If there are crops to be salvaged, the VC press into service all workers available and begin harvesting as soon after the spraying as possible in order to save the maximum amount of the crop. . . . Careful timing of the spraying mission denies the VC/NVA the opportunity to salvage any part of the crop. . . .

VC units also fear harmful physical effects as a result of spraying operations. This misconception on the part of VC/NVA troops developed as an adverse effect of an anti-herbicide propaganda campaign directed primarily toward civilians by the political cadre.

"Rice is the staff of life to the VC/NVA soldier," continues the report, and the majority of rice is

concentrated in the Mekong Delta area, where 68 percent of the annual rice crop is grown, I, II, and III Corps are rice deficient regions that must be supplied from the outside. This presents collection, storage and distribution problems for the enemy. . . . The destruction of crops in the fields, the capture of large rice caches, and the combination of defoliation and military operations have kept him on the move, reduced his source of supply, denied him access to his stores, and disrupted his distribution system.[12]

In addition to destroying food crops, the military wants to intensify its efforts to:

Reduce infiltration of NVA forces into SVN through Laos during the dry season. . . . *One promising technique is to contaminate certain selected interdiction points with riot control agent CS.* This agent has been approved for use in SVN and has been employed successfully in support of tactical operations. . . .

Riot control agents produce temporary irritating or disabling physiological effects when in contact with the eyes or when inhaled. Riot control agents used in field concentrations do not permanently injure personnel. Complete recovery from agent effects is spontaneous when the individual moves to a clear atmosphere.[13]

The use of passive voice, "This agent has been approved for use in SVN," is interesting. It is apparently okay for the military to use toxic gases against the enemy in Vietnam because someone, somewhere, approves of this tactic. Like herbicides, CS gas does not harm human beings. It might cause temporary "irritating or disabling" effects, but once individuals move to "a clear atmosphere" they will be fine.

Between October 1966 and April 1967, the military devises a new technique for destroying Vietnam's environment. It will send squadrons of B-52s over the defoliated jungle to firebomb "free strike targets" and square "target boxes" approximately seven kilometers on each side. Pilots will first saturate the jungle with Agent Orange, after which ground crews will make sure that the forest is dry enough to be ignited by incendiary bombs.

The director of defense research and engineering asks the Forest Service and the US Department of Agriculture to research the feasibility of destroying large areas of forest and jungle in Southeast Asia. (The declassified papers do not indicate what this research might entail).

On March 11, 1966, fifteen B-52 aircraft drop incendiaries on a defoliated area at Chu Phong Mountain near Pleiku. The results are "inconclusive"; however, the military decides that this "technique" might be "operationally feasible."[14]

Before the next phase begins, the Air Force flies 255 sorties over the experimental zone, expending 255,000 gallons of herbicides to kill the forests. The ground crews sent afterward find that the forest is dry, and thirty B-52s swarm over the target, dropping incendiary bombs on defoliated forests.

In its "Effectiveness of Burn" evaluation of these raids, the military concludes that open areas burn well, while "under double canopy, fires spread only about six feet on either side of ignition source.... Crown canopy removal negligible."

Smoke plumes rise 5,000 to 9,000 feet into the air after these raids, and enemy troops fire on the helicopters that attempt to survey the damage. Landing zones are most likely booby trapped, and the widespread fires the operation had hoped for do not occur.[15]

A team assigned to evaluate why Operation Pink Rose failed concludes:

> Density of bomblets was increased by a factor of three.
> Two additional months of maximum drying were provided.
> Timing between B-52 cells was reduced from four to three minutes to provide a more nearly simultaneous ignition. Vietnam refuses to burn.[16]

Many veterans believe that the military was experimenting with new weapon systems in Vietnam. In fact, they say, Vietnam was a dress rehearsal for future wars. The US and Great Britain perfected the tactic of firebombing cities in Europe and Japan during World War II, so it's only a matter of time before mad scientists discover how to set fire to entire nations, destroying all food supplies and killing anyone who doesn't flee the attack. Instant war. No contest. Over before it even starts.

In addition to the use of herbicides, the Air Force drops 3.5 million 500–700 pound bombs on Vietnam from 1967–68, leaving ten to fifteen million large craters, as well as many millions of unexploded munitions that will continue to wound and kill children, farmers, and others who collect scrap metal to sell after the war. The amount of energy these bombing raids release is the equivalent of 328 Hiroshima A-bombs...These attacks left some 10-15 million large bomb craters as a semi-permanent feature of the landscape in Vietnam, alone. Also left behind were many unexploded landmines, bomblets, and other unexploded ordinance (UXO) which continue to threaten life and limb throughout the region."[17]

The military also uses 2,500-pound Rome Plows to destroy Vietnam's forests. Nicknamed "Hog Jaws," just one of these massive bulldozers can clear 10,000 feet of trees up to eighteen inches in diameter every hour. Two tractors dragging a chain between them can rip out entire rows of rubber trees. Anyone caught hiding in the dense foliage will be shredded.[18]

Approximately 40 percent of the total forestlands in South Vietnam are damaged by shrapnel that leaves the trees susceptible to fungal entry and decay, killing many of these trees. Herbicides also damage the soil in Vietnam, destroying the microorganisms needed to prevent erosion and removing the humus material. This results in the soil turning lateritic, becoming rock hard.[19]

Vietnam's A Luoi Valley is particularly hard hit by defoliants. Before the war, this region was a tropical forest, rich in hardwoods, rare species of trees, and fauna. Elephants, gaur, tigers, panthers, sun bears, four species of pheasants, barking deer, wild boar, and monkeys roamed this tropical forest. The valley's rivers teemed with fish, a natural resource for local residents.

From 1966 to 1970, the US military sprays the valley repeatedly with Agent Orange, decimating the forests and killing large numbers of wild and domestic birds and mammals. According to Vo Guy, a Vietnamese expert on the environmental effects of Agent Orange, by 2005—thirty years later—there are no signs "that indigenous forest trees are growing in the A Luoi Valley."[20]

"The areas are still covered by wild weeds like many years ago," writes Vo Guy. "Fauna is very poor and different from the original. A comparison between A Luoi valley and two control forest areas, regarding numbers of bird species and small species, showed that only 24 bird species and 5 mammal species were found in A Luoi Valley, whereas 145 and 170 bird species and 30 and 55 mammal species were censured in these two control forests."[21]

At the height of the fighting, Dr. Arthur Westing, a scientist Dow Chemical considers one of the world's experts on dioxin, travels to Southeast Asia to assess the damage defoliants are inflicting on the environment and, consequently, on the people living in defoliated areas. In April 2002, Westing tells a symposium on Agent Orange at Yale University:

> Warfare is a human pastime the very intent of which is to subdue an enemy by inflicting upon it overpowering levels of death, destruction, and disruption. Damage to the human environment in time of war—both collateral and intentional—is thus as old as warfare itself (Westing, 1984a). Nonetheless, the Second Indochina War of 1961–1975 (the "Vietnam Conflict"; the "American War") stands out today as

the archetypical [sic] example of war-related environmental abuse. This negative image results from at least five major factors:

(a) Long-term systematic fury inflicted by one of the belligerents upon the environment of an enemy dependent for its survival upon a rural natural-resource-based economy (Westing 1976);

(b) The coincidence of this war with a widespread emergence of concern over the massive civil assaults being visited upon the global biosphere in general (Westing 1996a);

(c) The frightening medical consequences that have been associated with some of the environmental attacks (Westing 1978);

(d) Hostile atmospheric manipulations carried out by one of the belligerents (Westing 1976, 1977);

(e) A generalized morally or ethnically-based objection to this particular war or the way it was pursued by the USA.[22]

On January 22, 1975, President Gerald Ford announces that he has signed "instruments of ratification of the Geneva Protocol of 1925, and the biological Weapons Convention, to which the Senate gave its advice and consent on December 16, 1974." Mr. Ford decides:

that the United States shall renounce as a matter of national policy:

(1) first use of herbicides in war except use, under regulations applicable to their domestic use, for control of vegetation within J.S. bases and installations or around their immediate defense perimeters,

(2) first use of riot control agents in war except in defensive military modes to save lives, such as use of riot control agents in riot situations, to reduce civilian casualties, for rescue missions, and to protect rear area convoys.

This policy is detailed in the Executive order which I will issue today. The order also reaffirms our policy established in 1971 that any use in war of chemical herbicides and riot control agents must be approved by me in advance . . .

It is in my earnest hope that all nations will find it in their interest to join in this prohibition against biological weapons.[23]

In April 1969, the military releases a "Department of the Army Training Circular" stating: "ORANGE is relatively nontoxic to man and animals. No injuries have been reported to personnel exposed to aircraft spray. Personnel subject to splashes from handling the agent need not be alarmed, but should shower and change clothes at a convenient opportunity. ORANGE is noncorrosive to metals but will remove aircraft paint and walkway coatings. Contaminated aircraft should be washed with soapy water to remove the agent."[24]

In December 1969, the Council of the American Association for the Advancement of Science passes a resolution stating that:

Whereas, recent studies commissioned by the National Cancer Institute have shown that 2,4,5-T and 2,4-D cause birth malformations in experimental animals, and whereas, the above studies conclude that

2,4,5-T is probably dangerous to man, and that 2,4-D is potentially dangerous to man ...

Whereas, there is a possibility that the use of herbicides in Vietnam is causing birth malformations among infants of exposed mothers;

Therefore, be it resolved that the Council of AAAS urge that the US Department of Defense immediately cease all use of 2,4-D and 2,4,5-T in Vietnam.[25]

The defoliation campaign officially ends in 1970. However, the last American unit does not leave Vietnam until 1973, and it's hard to imagine that commanders will allow dense foliage to grow around their base camps, giving attackers cover to reach the perimeter without being detected. Perhaps American pilots do stop soaking the countryside with Agent Orange, but that does not mean that South Vietnam's Air Force stops flying spray missions, or that soldiers from South Korea, Australia, New Zealand, and the US stop spraying Agent Orange from backpacks, trucks, and helicopters. No one keeps track of the exact amounts of herbicide used this way.

Destroying large swaths of rice crops, fruit trees, and vegetable gardens causes widespread hunger among Vietnamese civilians. Peasants cultivate their own food, relying on methods of farming that their ancestors had practiced for generations: planting and harvesting rice, keeping chickens and ducks, catching fish and crabs in flooded paddies. There are no supermarkets, convenience stores, or fast food outlets in Vietnam's war-torn countryside, and even when food is available, families have to choose between eating poisoned crops and dying from hunger.

Today, when I ask combat veterans how the military managed to distinguish between "enemy" and "friendly" rice paddies, they shrug, as if to say "Come on, now. Nobody can be that stupid." Ground pounders are always smarter than the politicians who start wars and the generals who send soldiers into battle. It did not take long for GIs to realize that you do not win the hearts and minds of civilians by destroying their food crops. Mothers holding babies whose stomachs bulge with hunger hate the people responsible for killing their children. Fathers who are starving to death will want to hurt the people who are sending them to an early grave. I cannot imagine watching my own children waste away from hunger and, as they expire in my arms, being told that their suffering is for a noble cause.

No more herbicides in war, "except in a certain, very, very limited number of defense situations where lives can be saved."

President Ford did not explain what this caveat meant.

CHAPTER 2

Transformations

If I had my druthers, I would never speak of Vietnam. I'd just stay in my cave, read my books, and take care of my flowers. But I know that's not the reason I survived.

—George Mizo, co-founder, Friendship Village, Hanoi, Vietnam

HANOI, VIETNAM

We thread through narrow streets, past small shops selling fresh fruits and vegetables. I would like to stop for a Vietnamese iced coffee and talk to people who look so cool, even cheerful, in this brutal heat. Were they living in Hanoi during the war? This city is 1,000 years old. Can these shoppers trace their ancestry that far back?

We stop to buy bags of candy and other small gifts for the children. Our interpreter sits in the front seat beside the driver. They do not talk.

We arrived in Hanoi twenty-four hours after our flight lifted off from JFK, so jetlagged that we wandered like punch-drunk boxers about the airport. We were on the ground, in Vietnam, on the first leg of a research trip I'd been hoping to take for more than twenty years. When the taxi that we assumed the hotel would send failed to show, we accepted a ride with a couple of young men who couldn't understand where we wanted to go. I had expected a small city pockmarked with bomb craters and strewn with bits and pieces of downed American planes. However, Hanoi is a very large city, and there are no visible craters or bombed out buildings; there are no remnants of what the Vietnamese call "the American War."

We crossed the Song Hong (Red River), our new friends laughing at our delirium and trying to convince us to stay in "Uncle Dang's hotel." "Cheap," they said. "Very clean." From past experience, I knew that the Vietnamese are inveterate entrepreneurs, highly skilled at persuading tourists to spend money. "No thank you," I said. "Nice place. Very good to you." I did not know the Vietnamese word for "no." Somehow, they managed to locate our lodgings in the old city.

Our interpreter directs the taxi driver to stop at a small booth, exchanges a few words with a uniformed man, and we pass through an arch onto the grounds of The Friendship Village. Dang Vu Dung, director of the Village, greets us on the steps of the administration building. Inside, we drink bottled water and chat for a few minutes, but there are many visitors today and he apologizes for rushing off to meet with them.

On one wall of the main room is a large photograph of George Mizo, the combat veteran who returned to Vietnam to build a village that would care for children and adult victims of chemical warfare.

George looks uncomfortable in his shirt and tie, and there is a boyish shyness to his smile. I recall an exhibit of Richard Avedon's work at the Metropolitan Museum in New York. Huge photographs had been hung high on the walls to give viewers a sense of the subject's importance. Avedon had a genius for bringing out the worst in his subjects. Rich, famous, powerful people glared, even when attempting to appear cordial, with passionate disdain at the world. We were tempted to feel sorry for these people. We laughed. I'm not sure why.

Over the years, I'd spoken once or twice with George by phone, but had never gotten to know this man who had survived the killing fields of Southeast Asia and, seriously ill from his own exposure to Agent Orange, returned to Vietnam to create a place of healing, peace, and friendship. "A village," he said, "where ex-enemies could come together as friends. A living symbol," he hoped, "of the potential for human transformation."

George Mizo didn't have to fight in Vietnam. Honorably discharged from the United States Army in 1966, he could have stayed home and watched the war on television. But, as the limited conflict in Southeast Asia turned into a full-scale (undeclared) war, Mizo would remember the excitement he felt straddling his father's shoulders at a rally for presidential candidate Dwight D. Eisenhower.

"And my father said, 'These are the men who saved the free world. These are the men who stopped Hitler, Stalin, and the Japanese.'"

Beaming with pride for his country, George dreamed of the day that he would go off to fight for freedom in some foreign land, returning home with a chest full of medals and the thrill of a ticker-tape parade down New York's 5th Avenue.

One morning, about a year after he'd been honorably discharged from the army, George walked into a recruiting office, shook hands with the sergeant on duty, and informed him that he wanted to rejoin the army. At the time, Secretary of Defense Robert McNamara and other officials in the Johnson administration were exuding public confidence about the war. Troop morale in Vietnam was high, they said. The military was

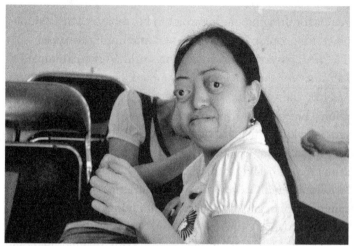

Girl working on a project in Friendship Village.

making progress, and the enemy was on the run. The recruiting sergeant did not tell new enlistees, because he had no way of knowing this, that US pilots were flying about eleven herbicide missions each day, destroying Vietnam's countryside, poisoning the water and food that US soldiers would consume while they were in the field.

George told the sergeant that before he signed any papers, he had two requests. One, he wanted to be in Vietnam within five days. Two, once he arrived he wanted to be assigned to a unit that was going to see a lot of combat.

"Well," George later told a film crew making a documentary about Friendship Village, "I got my wish on both counts."

Friendship Village is a cluster of well-kept buildings built upon what was once a rice paddy. There are classrooms, a clinic, and rooms where kids learn practical skills like sewing. We walk to a classroom where children are sitting around a table on which there are boxes of plastic objects like fruits and vegetables. Cinderella sprawls upon one wall, her yellow hair flowing long and beautiful. A small white dog licks the back of her hand, and a prince wearing a red cape stands by her side. A knight holding a large blue ax protects the prince, and a castle looms in the background, waiting for the happy couple to come inside, marry, and live happily ever after.

A fan whirs. The children do not talk, but some of the boys wrap themselves around Brendan, touching him, fondling his camera. He shakes hands with them, hugs them, takes their picture, and lets them photograph the room's walls and ceilings.

Unlike other children we will see on our journey, these kids appear to be fine, but then we notice that they are too quiet, poised, as though waiting to emerge from a trance. They sit upon their little chairs, expressionless, watching but not playing with their toys. Their fathers fought in rice paddies and jungles that were saturated with herbicides. Returning home from the war, they carried bullets and shrapnel in their bodies and the horrors of war in their minds. Surgeons would remove the bullets, time might help heal their minds, but TCDD-dioxin would remain in their fatty tissues for decades, harming their wives, deforming their offspring, and sending these ex-soldiers to early graves.

In the late 1960s, while the war still raged, Dr. Ton That Tung, one of the medical field's most prominent liver specialists, began research on the possible effects of Agent Orange on the North Vietnamese soldiers who served in southern provinces of Vietnam. These soldiers appeared to be fathering an excess number of children born with serious birth defects. Among the birth defects Dr. Tung and his colleagues observed were cleft lips, absence of nose and eyes, shortened limbs, malformed ears, club feet, absence of forearms, hydrocephaly (water on the brain) and anencephaly (a condition in which all or part of the brain is missing), and a variety of heart problems.

Because Dr. Tung was aware that laboratory research had already proven dioxin to be teratogenic and fetotoxic in female rats and mice, he was careful to inquire whether the wives of former North Vietnamese soldiers had been exposed to herbicides. Through interviews with veterans and their families, Tung's research team learned that *none of the women* who had given birth to deformed children were exposed to herbicides; yet in one district where the researchers found a total of nine birth defects out of two hundred and thirty-three births, all nine of the deformed children were fathered by veterans. In another district, where veterans comprised only a small percentage of the population, Dr. Tung found that veterans fathered half of the deformed children born during a four-year period. Six out of the thirty children born with defects were anencephalic, and veterans fathered all six.

Dr. Tung realized that his findings were extraordinary. In the region he was studying, there should have been:

> One anencephalia in every 2,777 births, whereas we have one anencephalia per 197.7 births among veterans from the south. Furthermore, we must emphasize the great number of cardiac deformities: 15 cases out of 43 defects, i.e., 34.8 percent of the defects. The involvement of the neural tube seems to be in agreement with the studies of Barbara Field, who proved that in Australia there is a linear relationship between the rising rate of *spina bifida* [a condition where the spine is improperly fused] in newborns in the *first generation* and the rate of 2,4,5-T utilized each year.[1]

Dr. Tung also found that the wives of exposed veterans had an abnormally high rate of miscarriages, premature births, and stillbirths, while an unusual number of the veterans suffered from sterility. The fathers of deformed children, writes Dr. Tung, exhibit "signs of direct contact with herbicidal sprays in South Vietnam."[2]

Concluding his paper, Dr. Tung writes:

> By comparing reproductive outcomes of Vietnamese soldiers exposed to Agent Orange and those who were not exposed, there appears to be an excess of birth defects in children of the exposed veterans. This suggests that dioxin may act as a mutagen and thus would represent the first example of teratogenic damage due to male exposure in humans.[3]

Unfortunately, Dr. Tung did not live to complete his research on the possible mutagenic effects of dioxin. His early research into the effects of Agent Orange on North Vietnamese soldiers and their offspring is a pioneering effort to determine the effects of chemical warfare on the Vietnamese people. If he were alive today, he would undoubtedly see the children in Friendship Village as a sad confirmation of his fear that dioxin might be a mutagenic chemical, and that men exposed to this chemical are likely to father an excessive number of deformed children.

On January 3, 1968, in an opening salvo of the Tet Offensive, North Vietnamese soldiers launched a furious attack on all three bases in the Que Son Valley. Wounded by one of the first rockets, George kept fighting through the night, and when medivac choppers arrived at dawn to pick up the dead and wounded, he refused to get on board until his commanding officer ordered him to do so.

George had seen many young men lose arms and legs or get carried away from firefights in body bags, and as the killing escalated and casualties mounted, he began to question the war.

"In the first few months, most of our battles centered around recapturing large plantations from the Vietcong. And I had no idea, none, that the United States had financial interests in Vietnam. I mean, I didn't know anything about Vietnam before I came there. None of us did. The American people didn't either.

"But I'd also come to realize that the Vietnamese are incredible people, very peaceful, with an ancient culture. And I couldn't understand why we were killing the very people and destroying the country I thought I'd come over to protect."

In spite of his doubts and serious injuries, Sergeant Mizo had insisted on remaining behind with his fellow soldiers: "I didn't want to leave. We came together. They were more than my men. They were my friends. My brothers."[4]

Yet at the height of the all-night battle, George experienced an epiphany: "For the first time I saw clearly. Everything stopped. It was like a movie. This isn't about democracy *versus* communism. This isn't about God's will. This is bullshit. This is a horror created by men, for whatever reason—politics or greed. We were killing the people and destroying the country we'd come to save. And at that moment, I knew that I would survive."

Later, recovering in a military hospital, George learned that the North Vietnamese had overrun his unit, killing his entire platoon.

"And that's when I made a conscious decision to stop being a soldier, and to actively oppose the war in Vietnam."[5]

In 1974, six years after he'd returned from Vietnam, George's

Boys in a classroom, Friendship Village.

skin broke out in a terrible rash, his temperature soared to 105°F, and he was delirious. He did not know it at the time, but like many of his brothers-in-arms, and like many of the soldiers they'd fought against, he was at the beginning of a long struggle to survive the ravages of Agent Orange/dioxin.

George heard stories about veterans whose wives were experiencing miscarriages, giving birth to lifeless babies, and to children with serious, sometimes horrific, birth defects. These ex-soldiers, still young, were suffering from cancer, debilitating skin rashes, growths that doctors diagnosed as precancerous, loss of sex drive, low sperm count, and other illnesses. When they'd gone off to fight in Vietnam, most still in their teens, they were in superb health; now, they seemed to be locked inside of a science fiction scenario, watching themselves turn, mysteriously, into old men.

These men served in different branches of the military, in different years (1961–73), and in different regions within the southern half of Vietnam. Most know nothing about Agent Orange, but do know that when they attempt to approach the Veterans Administration for help, officials there insist that very few US soldiers were exposed to toxic chemicals in Vietnam. Moreover, those who may have spent brief periods inside of spray zones have nothing to fear. There is absolutely no evidence, the Administration insists, that Agent Orange harms human beings.

The Department of Defense (DOD) informed veterans who asked for their service records that many had been lost during the chaotic evacuation of Saigon. Other records were destroyed in a fire in St. Louis, Missouri. Not to worry, said officials at the Veterans Administration. The Air Force kept computer-generated "Herb Tapes" of Ranch Hand missions and if veterans couldn't track their units' movements inside these grids, then they probably weren't exposed to Agent Orange. Soldiers who spent their tour of duty inside base camps would be fine; combat soldiers, said the DOD, did not enter jungles until six weeks after the trees were sprayed, so they had nothing to worry about.

Veterans who complained about illnesses—colon cancer, testicular cancer, liver and heart problems, and kidney disease—that normally do not affect men their age were told that they were alcoholics, drug addicts, malingerers, and suffering from combat stress.

Young women stitch beautiful scenes onto circles of white cloth. When you first see these children, you feel sad and empty, as though something true and good were turned upside down, shaken out of you. In the little shop you buy white hankies stitched with blue flowers, bookmarks with scenes from the countryside, perhaps a scarf or a tee shirt. You want to think that you are doing your part to care for these children, helping to heal the wounds of war.

According to Vietnamese officials, three million Vietnamese, including 500,000 children, are suffering from the effects of toxic chemicals used during the war. The exact number of retarded, blind, limbless, and paralyzed Vietnamese children isn't so important. What matters is that you will find these children in hospitals, community-run centers, and poor rural homes. You will be surprised, then amazed, then shocked by the abundance of Agent Orange children.

During the war years, or after, one or both of each Agent Orange child's parents were exposed to TCDD-dioxin, a chemical that Dr. Jacqueline Verrett of the Food and Drug Administration called "100,000 times more potent than thalidomide as a cause of birth defects in some species."[6]

One or both parents carry this deadly chemical in their fatty tissues.

In the study "Genetic Damage in New Zealand Vietnam War Veterans," researchers from Masey University in New Zealand write:

> Exposure to Agent Orange also has major effects on the reproductive system of humans; TCDD is an endocrine-disrupting chemical with a highly toxic effect on the human reproductive system.
>
> Even at low doses TCDD can seriously disrupt normal reproduction in humans; it can lower fertility, increasing antenatal mortality and the risk of endometriosis, and can also cause many birth defects.[7]

The New Zealand study concludes that a group of New Zealand veterans who served in Vietnam "has been exposed to

Children in a playroom, Friendship Village.

harmful substance(s) (TCDD-dioxin) which can cause genetic damage."[8]

In the late 1970s and early 1980s, a kind of collective, self-imposed amnesia washed over the United States. With the exception of the Civil War, Vietnam had been America's most divisive conflict. George Mizo realized that those who fought in and those who fought against the war might never reconcile their differences. Politicians and historians would write books, soldiers would write poetry, memoirs, and novels, Hollywood would try to make *the* Oscar-winning film about Vietnam. The Vietnamese would be blamed for the war, demonized, and forgotten.

George believed that he'd earned the right to speak out not just against the Vietnam War, but war itself. In 1986, George Mizo, Duncan Murphy, Brian Willson, and Medal of Honor winner Charles Litkey fasted for forty-seven days upon the steps of the nation's capitol to protest US involvement in

Nicaragua. George talked about the Nuremberg Principles that, he said, obligate citizens to take direct action if and when their government violates international law. He spoke about his love and respect for the Vietnamese people; the government that sent him to kill and possibly die in Vietnam now sent him to prison for his anti-war actions.

George knew he was living on borrowed time, and he wanted to leave a legacy of peace to a people he'd learned to respect and love. So he and a few friends decided to create a community for Agent Orange victims in Vietnam. Friendship Village would be about hope, healing, and reconciliation. It would be a place where children and Vietnamese veterans suffering from exposure to Agent Orange could live in a caring, comfortable, loving environment.

Friendship Village, said George, "would be a living symbol

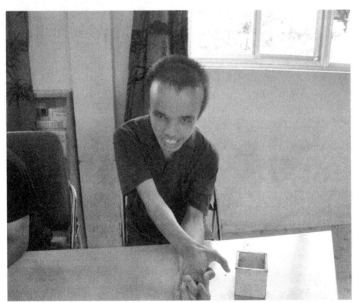

Young man in Friendship Village.

of the potential for transformation. And it would show that people can make a difference."

George Mizo died around the time that the Mount Sinai School of Medicine's Center for Children's Health and the Environment released a series of reports on the effects of chemicals like dioxin on young children.

In one article, "Johnny Can't Read, Sit Still, or Stop Hitting the Neighbor's Kid. Why?" researchers write:

> Studies show that lead, mercury, industrial chemicals, and certain pesticides cross the placenta and enter the brain of the developing fetus where they can cause learning and behavioral disabilities. This is true in young animals—and in young children.[9]

Researchers have discovered DDT (long banned in the United States), as well as other toxic chemicals—heptachlor, chlordane, mirex, dieldrin, benzene, and chloroform—in mothers' milk.

> We know that during gestation and in the early months after birth, an infant's brain is particularly susceptible to harm from toxic chemicals. We don't know what the minimum safe levels of exposure are. It may be that no exposure is safe .... We know that occupational exposure to PCBs, dioxin, and other POPs has been linked to several cancers and to a broad range of reproductive problems, including birth defects in offspring.[10]

At the grand opening of Friendship Village in October 1998, Lt. General Tran Van Quang, the officer who planned and fought in the battle that seriously wounded George Mizo and killed his entire unit, joined Vice President Madam Binh and George in the ribbon-cutting celebration. Through years of planning and trying to raise money for Friendship Village, George and General Quang had become close friends. On October 30, 2000, George Mizo, his wife Rosi Hohn-Mizo, and George Doussin of France were awarded Vietnam's first ever State Medal of Friendship. After the ceremonies, General Vo 'Nguyen Giap, senior military commander during the French and American wars, met privately with the recipients. General Giap, a man who'd spent his entire life fighting for Vietnam's independence, took twelve-year-old Michael Mizo in his arms.

"Michael," he said. "Never go to war."

Soon after George Mizo died at his home in the village of Hofen, Germany, on March 18, 2002, his wife and son sent out a message of love for the man who'd devoted his life to helping victims of chemical warfare: "Peace is giving something to life . . . Your spirit is living in our hearts and in the Vietnam Friendship Village."

One of the boys in the classroom, a twenty-one-year-old man in a seven-year-old child's body, picks up a shape, stares at it for a minute, then drops it back into the bowl. Other children stare at the shapes, expecting them, it seems, to come alive.

"Yes," says their teacher. "Those are puzzles. It's hard for these children. Sometimes it takes them a year to solve one."

As our taxi navigates Hanoi's crowded streets, Brendan and I discuss how we'd like to use his photographs. We do not wish to portray these children as freaks of nature. Nor do we intend to exploit their physical handicaps and mental deficiencies. We have fallen in love with the children at Friendship Village, not out of pity, but because they are beautiful human beings.

Chemical warfare has left them with deformities and limited intelligence, but it did not—and cannot—strip them of their humanity.

CHAPTER 3

Promises

The United States has renounced the first use of incapaci-
tating chemical weapons.
 The United States has renounced any use of biological
and toxin weapons.

—Richard M. Nixon, August 19, 1970

HANOI, VIETNAM

Another broiling day on the streets of Hanoi: women squat-
ting on the sidewalk, peeling coconuts, cutting up jackfruit,
slicing pineapples; early morning clumps of people seated on
tiny stools, dipping chopsticks into bowls of noodles; a million
motorbikes and taxis honking in a mad, cacophonic, yet somehow orderly rush to reach their destinations. Hanoi, capital of
a united Vietnam, city of lakes, pounded for years by waves of
fighter planes and B-52s, the resting place of Ho Chi Minh,
who lies in a mausoleum guarded by stone-faced Vietnamese
soldiers wearing starched white uniforms.

 In Hanoi, Water Puppets dressed in bright Vietnamese cos-
tumes fight dragons, go fishing, and clash in maritime battles.
Beautiful women at outdoor markets sell fresh fruits and vegetables, shrimp, and dog meat. Little stands sell glasses of
fresh-squeezed sugar cane juice, and it's a short cab ride from

the old city to Hoalo Prison, a dark, dreary, miserable sprawl of dungeons built by the French in 1896 to hold those Vietnamese accused of resisting colonialism. From August 5, 1964 to March 13, 1973, American fliers shot down over Hanoi and the surrounding regions were held in Hoalo prison, which they jokingly called "the Hanoi Hilton."

We pass Hoan Kiem Lake, where people of all ages gather at dawn to stroll together, stretch to music, and perform gentle dance routines—each one with its own style. Waving bright red fans, groups of women practice Tai Chi, while other early risers pray or meditate. Residents of Hanoi seem to agree with Ho Chi Minh's philosophy that exercise is a good means of maintaining physical and mental health.

Legend has it that in the fifteenth century, King Le Loi was boating on this green lake when a great tortoise rose from the water, took a magical sword from the king's belt, and swam into the depths to return the sword to the Dragon King. A two-story structure with pointed Gothic arches and a tiled cupola appears to float upon the lake. Thap Rua, or Turtle Tower, honors the magic turtle that still guards King Le Loi's sword. At one point during their sixty-four-year-long occupation of Vietnam, French colonialists placed a model of the Statue of Liberty on top of Turtle Tower. Resistance fighters responded by hoisting the revolutionary flag next to Lady Liberty. When the Tran Trong Kim government assumed control of the city in 1945, the statue came down.

By the time we reach the top of the stairs, we are guzzling water and drowning in sweat. Dr. Prof. Nguyen Trong Nhan greets us with the unassuming courtesy that Vietnamese show visitors. From 1954 until recently, Dr. Nhan was the director at this hospital where he now maintains a two-room office. "Now," he laughs, "I can try to get something done."

An assistant brings iced Vietnamese coffee, and we settle into chairs across from a huge mural of the snow-clad Rocky Mountains.

"You see, George H. Bush," smiles Dr. Nhan, pointing to a photograph in which he stands next to George W. Bush's father. "And Bill Clinton," he says, gesturing to a picture of himself and President Clinton. Ho Chi Minh also adorns Dr. Nhan's walls, but a good distance away from the two American presidents.

In a smaller room piled high with books and papers, there's a black and white photo of four handsome young men.

"My brothers. I'm on the right. Twenty-three years old, in Division 312, which began and finished the battle of Dienbienphu. Before the battle began, I was sent to study in medical school. At the center, that's my cousin from Division 308. He died in the battle at Dienbienphu. The center, low, is my young brother from Division 320, and he died in North Delta. He was twenty years old and the doctor of a battalion. On the left, that's my older brother from Division 308. He died from disease in Hanoi after the victory at Dienbienphu.

"We all served in our Vietnam People's Army during the war against French aggression. All my brothers were more intelligent than me, and they died. During the war against US aggression, I worked as a doctor in Hanoi. Only in 1976, after the victory on April 30, 1975, did I visit the south."

At the International Conference of Victims of Agent Orange/Dioxin, Hanoi, March 2006, Dr. Nhan, acting as vice president of the Vietnam Association for Victims of Agent Orange, (VAVA), spoke about Vietnam's long struggle for independence, the nation's remarkable recovery and development, and the fact that Vietnam and its people continue to suffer from "severe war wounds left behind by the largest chemical warfare in mankind's history."[1]

Dr. Nhan went on to say that in the early 1970s, "researchers from Harvard University found high levels of dioxin in Vietnamese mothers' breast milk." Thirty-five years later, Professor Arnold Schecter and his Vietnamese counterpart, Prof. Le Cao Dai, discovered high levels of dioxin in Vietnamese living near a former military zone and in the fatty tissues of Vietnamese Agent Orange victims.

Most "painful and dangerous," said Dr. Nhan, "is that dioxin infects not only one generation, but also several. Despite the war already ended [*sic*] for more than thirty years, we have witnessed severe congenital malformation. . . . It is worth noting that in the years of the 1990s, the studies done by certain US scientists found the presence of dioxin in the sperm of the Vietnam-American veterans. This explains the toxicities of the male productive cell deformities. During pregnancy and after birth, dioxin in blood and milk continues to harm fetus, and newborn."[2]

On August 6, 2004, Dr. Nhan forwarded *To The American People, an Open Letter*, asking Americans to support the Vietnamese class action lawsuit charging the chemical manufacturers of Agent Orange with war crimes.

"With sincere and friendly sentiments, from a far-away land of the West Pacific Ocean," the letter opens, "we would like to send this letter to all of you. It is written on the pending day of August 10, when the US aircrafts, in 1961, began the spraying of herbicides in Vietnam with the northern areas of Kontum as their first target."[3]

In 2006, the *Anthropology Review* published a special issue on "Victims of Agent Orange/Dioxin in Vietnam," in which contributor Le Thi writes: "According to statistics of Kontum General Hospital in 1999, there were 12 defect or monstrous births. Popular [most frequent] cases are children born without anus, or chest or belly-linked twins. Some children were born without belly skin and all their intestines and livers are exposed. The highest number of birth defects is seen in the two districts *of Sa Thay* and *Dak To.*"

In the same article, Dr. Nguyen Anh Tu, from Kontum Provincial Health Department, discusses the cases he has seen:

> Mrs. Nguyen Thi Tra is from Trung Dung village. In 1979, she gave birth to a big bundle containing dust particles. In the same year, Mrs. Nguyen Thi Nho from Hoa Binh village (Sa Nghia Commune) gave birth to a bundle full of eggs.... In the northern province of Thai Binh, there are now 20,000 victims of Agent Orange. In Quynh Phu district alone, 8,000 people are Agent Orange victims, including 129 are from the third generation. Mr. Nguyen Bach Le in Quynh Hoang Commune took part in the battlefields of Quang Tri. He got married after being demobilized. His son, Nguyen Ba Hau, is now 35 years old but he is only 1 meter tall, with very short limbs. Hau is now married. His first son is normal but his second son is defected like him. His second son is now 12 years old but is only eighty cm tall with a distorted face. In Mr. Le's family, three generations have been affected by Agent Orange.[4]

Le Thi writes about an ex-soldier whose first child went blind when he was one month old, and who grew up severely retarded; a second child "looks monstrous," his legs, (one long, one short) shrinking, his hands "very long and thin." A third child is also a "monster" who looks exactly like his younger brother.

"In my family," said the children's father, "there is always a fight with my children screaming all the night. After nearly 30 years since peace has been restored in the country, we have not experienced a single day of peace."[5]

Another soldier returned to his native village and got married after the war. In 1977, his wife gave birth to a "7-month headless and limbless foetus whose eyes are on his neck. Her second birth was a piece of pink flesh looked like worms intertwining together. Her third monstrous birth was a hairy monkey and the fourth one was a bundle of tumors."[6]

In another case, a soldier's wife gave birth to a child with two faces. This child died after three months.

> Their second child had a pig face and their third child a mouse face. All of them died after birth. The fourth child was born normal, but when it was 8 months old, its face became red and died. Their fifth child, a normal son, but suffering from mental disorder, screaming all the times and tearing everything he can. He even bit his own body to satisfy his craziness. He is 23 years old now with Mrs. Tuu caring for him throughout all those years. She said: "I have nothing in my life, except tears."[7]

From the early days of the defoliation campaign, Dr. Nhan explained, scientists tried to warn of the possible consequences of using herbicides in Vietnam. Many prestigious American and world researchers opposed the spraying, including Professor Arthur Galston, a biologist at Harvard, the US Physiobotanist Association, and 5,000 other US scientists, including seventeen Nobel laureates and 129 members of the US National Academy of Sciences.

"The war is over," writes Dr. Nhan in his *Open Letter to the*

American People, "but while the country has made remarkable progress since the fighting ended, millions of people are suffering from incurable diseases related to exposure to dioxin. Thousands of people have already died in agony with deep indignation towards the perpetrators of crimes. Many women have suffered reproductive complications and even the total loss of the right to be a mother."[8]

The letter expresses sorrow that children who had nothing to do with the war will be "born with inherited diseases, and, of course, without the smallest hope of enjoying even a minute of happiness of living like an ordinary being. The victims of Agent Orange/dioxin are the most miserable and tragic people. Many of them, with lots of deformed offspring, have barely survived in poverty."[9]

The Vietnam Association for Victims of Agent Orange (VAVA) wants the American people to know that the Vietnamese "thirst for peace and friendship, and have exerted great patience, hoping the United States will cooperate in solving the cruel war consequences, especially those severe evils resulting from horrible chemical warfare."[10]

Faced with the US government's intransigence and apparent indifference to their plight, the Vietnamese people were forced to file a lawsuit against companies that "gained enormous profits from the sufferings of millions of people."

Agent Orange advocates like Dr. Nhan want people to know that the lawsuit is designed not just to help Vietnamese people, but other victims of Agent Orange as well, including veterans in the United States, Australia, the Republic of South Korea, Thailand, New Zealand, and the Republic of the Philippines.

The Vietnam Association for Victims of Agent Orange concludes its letter by assuring its former adversary that the

Vietnamese have "never harbored any sense of hatred for the American people. . . . The present struggle is directly aimed at the peaceful and happy life of our future generations on this planet."[11]

Long before the American war ended, Dr. Nhan began to notice that people who'd lived or fought in defoliated areas of Vietnam experienced more difficulty recovering from illnesses than those who had remained in the North during the fighting. Patients suffering from a single ailment generally recovered; however, other patients deteriorated rapidly, and no remedy could be found to restore them to health. Something was undermining these terminally ill patients' immune systems. After careful study, Dr. Nhan concluded that many people had been exposed to dioxin, and that this chemical was killing them.

Certain that millions of Vietnamese people were suffering from the legacies of chemical warfare, Dr Nhan established the fund for Agent Orange victims in 1998. That fund now belongs to VAVA. He also realized that the symptoms of Agent Orange illness are similar to HIV, and he learned that President Clinton wanted to help victims of AIDS.

"So you see, when President Clinton came to Vietnam in 2000, I said to him that Agent Orange sickness is very similar to AIDS. Later, in his letter to me, Mr. Clinton agreed that we should engage in humanitarian activities, and that we ought to develop cooperation between our two countries to help Agent Orange victims.

"After that, he established a foundation to help Vietnam fight against the spread of AIDS. But he did not help Agent Orange victims. I asked him, 'Why won't you help us? You agree with me that we should have cooperation and humanitarian activities between our two countries, to help Agent Orange victims. But now you don't want to help these victims? Why not?'

"I explained that like AIDS victims, people who've been

exposed to Agent Orange suffer from immune deficiency. So why wouldn't he help Agent Orange victims who suffer from the same thing as people who are sick and dying from AIDS?

"I can show you on my computer that I have many emails between me and President Clinton. Did he answer my questions? No, he did not."

"Why didn't President Clinton answer your questions?" I asked him.

"Can you agree with me to have a frank answer?" he replied.

"That is exactly why we are in Vietnam, to ask questions and to receive frank answers."

"Okay. President Clinton, when he was the US president, was very afraid. You know, before becoming president of the US, he didn't enter the army. So, he lifted the embargo and established normal relations with Vietnam, but you see that's all he could do for this country. You know, the Agent Orange issue is very sensitive. It is a war crime. President Clinton did not want to get involved with a war crime.

"He didn't understand that Vietnam wants to have good relations with the US. We had already helped the US Army find the remains of soldiers here in Vietnam."

Dr. Nhan looks at the photographs on his walls, as though hoping that Mr. Clinton might say that he's sorry to have reneged on his promise. He will order his staff to look into ways that the United States might help Vietnamese Agent Orange victims. He will create a fund specifically for impoverished Agent Orange families. He will . . .

Iced Vietnamese coffee is delicious. I'd like another. Our translators and other people who accompany us to and from these interviews do not ask for, and will not accept anything but water.

"*Missing in action*," says Dr. Nhan, switching to English,

then back to Vietnamese. "If the Vietnamese people are willing to help find these war victims, why shouldn't the US help
us with our own war victims? If the US will just accept our
proposal to help victims, then there will be no more lawsuits."

"No more lawsuits?" I ask.

"Yes, no more lawsuits. At the meeting I had with President
Clinton in Hanoi, I told him why we want to establish a
humanitarian relationship between the US and Vietnam, but
the United States did not reply to our demands. They did help
us find the remains of some Vietnamese war victims, but they
did not help us with Agent Orange. Not at all."

When he was president of Vietnam's Red Cross, Dr. Nhan
convinced the American Red Cross to help Agent Orange victims and that organization agreed to give Vietnam $1 million.

"And since there are at least three million victims," he laughs,
"that means that each victim would get about thirty cents. You
cannot eat very much in Vietnam with that amount of money.

"And yes, some days ago we were informed that the Obama
administration is willing to contribute $3 million. So now we have
gathered $6 million altogether for cleaning up Vietnam's envi-
ronment, and for helping every Agent Orange victim in Vietnam.

Dr. Nhan pauses to make sure that we get the joke. Brendan wanders around the room, taking photographs. The
interpreters write in their notebooks.

"That would mean," he says, speaking in English to empha-
size the irony, "that each victim would receive $2.00. Can you visit
Vietnam with $2.00? Can you eat breakfast in Hanoi for $2.00?"

"Can't even get a taxi in Hanoi for $2.00," I reply, and we all
laugh, knowing that taxi drivers in this city are notorious for
overcharging their fares.

Dr. Nhan looks at the snow-covered slopes of the Rocky
Mountains, so quiet, cool, inviting.

"The Obama administration have very good humor," he chuckles. "Very good humor. And Obama has not visited Vietnam, so perhaps he thinks Vietnamese are not intelligent people.

"When I was the president of the Red Cross, I promised the victims of Agent Orange that if I can not do anything during that time, in some humanitarian way for them, I will support them all the way to appealing the lawsuit in the United States.

"That's why in 2004, they asked me to be vice president of VAVA, and to work on behalf of the Agent Orange victims' fight for justice. Our job is to support the lawsuit, and to mobilize support for victims in our country and abroad.

"In 2005, I went to the United States and traveled to ten of its biggest cities, where I met a lot of American people. And I informed them about the truth of the suffering in Vietnam. I met professors as well as students in many famous cities like Washington, Chicago, Seattle, and San Francisco. I don't remember all of them."

In October, 2008, the American Studies Association invited Dr. Nhan to address their annual meeting in Albuquerque, New Mexico. Unwilling to make such an arduous trip, he sent the conference a copy of his paper, "Agent Orange and the Conscience of the USA," which he began by telling the scholars that as a boy he was quite curious about America.

> At that time, like any other little boy, I was not interested in politics, but enjoyed watching American movies like the cartoon *Snow White and the Seven Dwarfs*, *Pinocchio*, and cowboy films. We enjoyed American movies not because of the scenes of riding and shooting, but their happy endings, which mean

"the good defeats the evil." And I longed naively to see America! But now the US has come to Vietnam.[12]

Dr. Nhan told the delegates how, following the Geneva Agreement in 1954 that divided Vietnam along the 17th parallel, the United States decided to mount a campaign to destroy Vietnam's independence movement. "Ten years later, my boyish, naïve hope was completely broken when the US Air Forces bombed the North of Vietnam, threatening to 'bring it back to the Stone Age.'"

Herbicides destroyed "more than three million hectares of forest. . . . As a consequence, erosion, floods and droughts seriously damaged the agriculture—the main means of existence of the majority of the Vietnamese people."

"Vietnamese women," he says,

have experienced disorders and complications during pregnancy, including miscarriages, still births, premature births, and severe fetal malformations. These reproductive problems have deprived many women of their right to be a mother. . . .

The most painful fact is that dioxin affects generations. The rate of children who have congenital malformations in Vietnam is higher than that in other countries even thirty years after the war ended. . . . It's a pity that American judges have dismissed the claims of Vietnamese Agent Orange victims with very unconvincing reasons. In fact, they don't respect the truth and justice.[13]

In January 2006, a Seoul court ordered Dow Chemical and Monsanto to pay $62 million to 6,800 Korean veterans and

their families. New Zealand's government apologized for sending its veterans to Southeast Asia where they were exposed to
dioxin. New Zealand's Vietnam veterans were planning to file
a lawsuit against the US chemical companies claiming $3 bil-
lion in compensation.

> The courageous struggle of the Agent Orange victims
> in Vietnam and their lawsuit are not only for the sake
> of their own and their children, but also for the legit-
> imate benefit of the Agent Orange victims in other
> countries such as America, Korea, Australia, New
> Zealand, and Canada.[14]

Dr. Nhan concluded his talk by asking the scholars whether
there is justice and conscience in the USA? And, if so, who
might the people be who really respect it?

Dr. Nhan offers me another cup of coffee. "Do you know
Admiral Zumwalt and his book, *My Father, My Son*?" he asks.
"Yes, I do know Admiral Zumwalt."
As the officer in command of all naval operations in the
southern half of Vietnam, Admiral Zumwalt ordered the use
of Agent Orange along the banks of rivers and canals. His
son, Lieutenant Elmo Zumwalt III, served on one of boats
that plied these waterways, searching for Vietcong to kill.
During lulls in the fighting, he and his crew swam in the
Quang Nam and Ma rivers, ate food from markets along
riverbanks, and drank water contaminated with Agent
Orange. Lieutenant Zumwalt and I were scheduled to appear
together on "Kelly & Company," a live audience talk show in
Detroit. Unfortunately, he was terminally ill and couldn't fly
to Michigan, so he called into the show and we talked

together that way. A man sat in a wheelchair in the front row of the studio. He was holding a photograph of a nineteen-year-old soldier. Now in his early thirties, the ex-soldier who'd been exposed to Agent Orange was a trembling, emaciated, feeble old man.

Elmo Zumwalt III fathered a son with learning disabilities and, after a long, hard struggle he died of cancer.

Admiral Zumwalt spent the last years of his own life advocating for Agent Orange victims. After an exhaustive study to determine whether "it is as likely as not that there is a statistical association between exposure to Agent Orange and a specific health effect," Zumwalt concluded that the government *and* the chemical companies had in fact conspired to deny Vietnam veterans much needed help for their war-related illnesses. Perhaps his most disturbing finding was that some notable "scientific studies" were seriously flawed or falsified, with researchers using bogus statistics to deny any association between exposure to Agent Orange and human illness:

> For instance, recent litigation against the Monsanto Corporation revealed conclusive evidence that studies conducted by Monsanto employees to examine the health effects of exposure to dioxin were fraudulent. These same fraudulent studies have been repeatedly cited by government officials to deny the existence of a relationship between health problems and exposure to Agent Orange.[15]

Even before beginning his research, Admiral Zumwalt knew that Ranch Hand pilots, who flew C-123 aircraft to defoliate Vietnam's forests and jungles, had been heavily exposed to Agent Orange. He was also aware that based on its Ranch

Hand study, the Air Force had concluded that Agent Orange had not adversely affected these pilots. Zumwalt's research confirmed his suspicions that this study was seriously flawed.

> In 1987, Ranch Hand scientists confirmed to Senator Daschle that an unpublished birth defects report shows that birth defects among Ranch Hand children are double those of children in the control group and not "minor" as originally reported in 1984.[16]

Ranch Hander pilots "also showed a significant increase in skin cancers unrelated to overexposure to the sun as originally suggested in the 1984 report."[17]

And:

> The Centers for Disease Control (CDC) birth defects study was confined to Vietnam Veterans located in the Atlanta, Georgia region. The study was not an Agent Orange birth defects study since no effort was made to determine whether the veterans had ever been exposed to Agent Orange.[18]
>
> For the Airforce to have made the statement in 1990 of no evidence of a link between exposure to Agent Orange and the cancer problems experienced by Ranch Handers is, as Senator Daschle notes, "patently false."[19]

Admiral Zumwalt chastised the Veterans' Advisory Committee on Environmental Hazards for its "blanket lack of impartiality. In fact, some members of the Advisory Committee and other VA officials have, *even before reviewing the evidence* [my italics], publicly denied the existence of a correlation between exposure to dioxin and adverse health effects."[20]

Zumwalt concluded that there was ample scientific evidence to demonstrate a connection between Agent Orange exposure and human illness. Regarding the question of birth defects, he wrote:

> Any Vietnam Veteran, or Vietnam Veteran's child who has a birth defect, should be presumed to have a service-connected health effect if that person suffers from the type of health effects considered with dioxin exposure and the Veteran's health or service record establishes 1) abnormally high TCDD in blood tests; or 2) the veteran's presence within 20 kilometers and 30 days of a known sprayed area (as shown by HERBs tapes and corresponding company records); or 3) the Veteran's presence at fire base perimeters or brown water operations where there is reason to believe Agent Orange [spraying] has occurred.[21]

Admiral Zumwalt confirmed that Vietnam veterans suffering Agent Orange exposure had been right all along.

In his address to American Study scholars in Albuquerque, Dr. Nhan quotes President Clinton:

> [Clinton said,] "Today we are showing that America can listen and act. Our country can face up to the consequences of our actions.... We will bear the responsibility for the harm we do, even when the harm is unintended.... Nothing we can do will ever repay the Vietnam veterans for all they gave and all they lost, particularly those who have been damaged by Agent Orange."[22]

President Clinton promised to *listen* to victims of Agent Orange. He did not promise to help them secure quality health care. Nor did he offer them financial assistance. The key word in the president's speech is "unintended."

Outside, the honking grows, expands, echoes off buildings, bounces into the room; it is so discordant that a Vietnamese English-language paper publishes an indignant editorial protesting against "Hanoi's Horny Drivers."

Our translators check their notes, and Dr. Nhan talks about the Vietnamese lawsuit, which US appellate courts have dismissed and which the Supreme Court refused to even discuss.

"At the beginning, we didn't think we could win the case. You see, in some wars we lost, but finally we were the winner. So we will have many ways outside of the court to struggle against the chemical companies."

We've been talking a long time and the interpreters must be tired. Sometimes, we have to stop and sort things out because we are attempting to communicate across cultural and linguistic differences. In English, we use "go," "going," "gone, " while the Vietnamese speak and write in what we call the present tense. In Vietnamese, a sequence of letters has only one meaning, but depending on the tone a speaker uses, the meaning of these letters changes. There's no simple use of "you," and there seems to be no real place, as in English, for "I."

Once, *I* was telling some Vietnamese friends about the time a policeman in Washington, DC broke my leg, shattering my kneecap with his nightstick, and—as I lay curled into a ball of agony—he threatened to kill me. Everyone laughed. I laughed as well, assuming that the translator's intonation had turned my sad tale into an amusing one. On another occasion in Ho Chi Minh City, across from the Continental Hotel, a bedraggled young man offered to shine my sneakers.

He complained that he did not have any money, he was hungry, and he wanted to return home to Hanoi. When I handed him 50,000 đồng, he grew tense. "Why do you give me đồng?" he demanded. "Because I wanted to," I said. He walked away in a huff.

Dr. Nhan has lived through decades of colonialism and war. His hopes soared when Ho Chi Minh, speaking before a massive crowd in Hanoi on September 2, 1945, quoted from the United States Declaration of Independence. Surely, the Americans would support Uncle Ho's new government. Instead, the French launched a violent campaign to recolonize Vietnam. Before France was finally forced to leave Vietnam for good, the United States was paying for eighty percent of its campaign to remain in Vietnam.[23]

After the Geneva Agreement in 1954, it seemed that the Vietnamese would soon choose their own president and live in peace in a united Vietnam. But the Eisenhower administration, convinced that Ho Chi Minh was a communist and fearing the loss of valuable assets in Indochina, sent General Edward Lansdale to Saigon to set up a "dirty tricks" squad— covert action teams that would seek to sabotage transportation networks in the north, counterfeit Vietminh documents, and spread rumors that there would be terrible massacres if Ho Chi Minh became president.

Lansdale helped Ngo Dinh Diem, a Catholic Mandarin, return to power in Saigon, and he set up the Saigon Military Mission to train Diem's army. The American War had begun. It would last for twenty years.

During the American War, Dr. Nhan worked as a surgeon in Hanoi. One day, while operating on a patient, he looked out the window to see bombs falling. Children and the elderly had been evacuated from Hanoi, but hospital staff kept working while B-52s rained death upon the city.

"I can not say if it's a short or long time for the US side or the chemical companies to admit this matter," says Dr. Nhan, "but I think they have to admit their responsibility for what they did in Vietnam, and the consequences for the Vietnamese people.

"The Vietnamese people want to close the past. You know, even US veterans, when they come to visit Vietnam, they receive a warm welcome from Vietnamese people. And they have a good time in Vietnam.

"And you know that in the past, the Japanese committed crimes in Vietnam. During World War II, after the Japanese invasion, about two million Vietnamese were suffering from hunger. But we don't talk about that story. Up to now, Japan is one country that has helped us a lot."

Dr. Nhan is convinced that the $180 million out of court settlement benefited US veterans. It's difficult to imagine that such a large sum of money would not assure that veterans, their families, and their widows would be taken care of. But when a reporter for *Thanh Nien News* asked attorney Gerson H. Smoger how the chemical companies could "get away with compensating Americans but not Vietnamese," he replied:

> I would not say that they "got away with compensating," because I can assure you that the responsible chemical companies had no interest in compensating anyone. Also, unfortunately, the chemical companies have never really compensated the vast majority of American veterans either. While there was a settlement entered into in 1984, the money ran out in 1994. Of the 2.4 million Americans who served in Vietnam,

only about 60,000 ever received anything from the companies. . . . Given how long it takes to get cancer from the chemicals, virtually none of the veterans who got cancer have received any compensation from the companies.[24]

When American courts dismissed the Vietnamese lawsuit, says Dr. Nhan, many people in other countries such as Australia, Korea, and New Zealand also lost. In New Zealand, Agent Orange victims asked for compensation of $3 billion. And the number of Agent Orange victims is much smaller than in Vietnam.

"When I was in the United States, I met a lot of Vietnam veterans. They were angry at their government because it did not recognize the effects of dioxin on their children and their wives. But the United States knows more about the consequences of dioxin on people. They keep it a secret."

"A secret?" I ask him.

"Yes, that's right. A secret."

Our taxi driver weaves in and out of a sea of motorbikes, honking as he narrowly misses—it seems to us—knocking riders from their seats. Hanoi's streets twist and turn, so it often feels as though we are going in circles. Sometimes, we are.

We swing by the lake in which 500-year-old tortoises reside, happy to know that they can bask in the sun without worrying about bombs. Every morning at six a.m., *Radio Hanoi* begins the day with a lyrical song.

> *Wherever we find ourselves in the four points of the compass*
> *Our hearts are turned to Ha Noi*

Ha Noi, the capital city so dear to us,
Once showered with bombs, now in peace
We recall the old dormant streets,
The shade trees, the chorus of cicadas at noon in
summer,
The newly built parks where the young grass
Is not yet marked by the traces of your steps
The Sword Lake with its blue waters
Where is mirrored the slanted shadow of the Tortoise
Stupa.[25]

CHAPTER 4

Sprayed and Betrayed

The story of Agent Orange is the story of technology run amok and turned upon its creators.

—Senator John Kerry

MAY 7, 1984, BROOKLYN, NEW YORK

Lawyers who represent Vietnam veterans and their families agree to a $180 million out-of-court settlement with the chemical companies that manufactured and sold Agent Orange to the military during the war. Outraged, veterans and their supporters call the settlement a "sellout," denouncing the attorneys who made the agreement without notifying all of the plaintiffs, and they vow to keep fighting for justice for Agent Orange victims.

With this out-of-court settlement, Dow, Monsanto, et al. win a monumental battle. They have prevented the veterans from arguing—and more importantly from winning—their case in court.

The five companies that continue to manufacture phenoxy herbicides claim that their products are perfectly safe. But if herbicides like 2,4,5-T and 2,4-D do not in fact harm human beings, the US veterans ask, then why are veterans from Korea, New Zealand, and Australia, who were similarly exposed to these chemicals, suffering from serious ailments? Why are so many of their children born with serious birth defects? The Vietnamese people have been complaining for years about the effects of Agent Orange on their farm animals and on their families. One day they too will file a class action lawsuit charging the manufacturers of Agent Orange with war crimes.

Veterans and their families are not asking for government handouts, and—contrary to the media coverage of this case, which is the largest product liability lawsuit in American history—they are not hoping to win large sums of money. What they really want is to show the world what happens to human beings who are exposed to deadly chemicals like dioxin. Veterans want people to know that as soldiers in Vietnam they drank water and ate food contaminated with Agent Orange/dioxin. They crawled through, bathed in, and even slept in water that had been sprayed with Agent Orange. They were doused with it when aircraft returning to base after defoliation missions jettisoned their loads.

Doctors at Veterans Administration hospitals call these veterans crazy and accuse them of being alcoholics, drug addicts, and malingerers, filing false claims in order to secure disability payments. The US government denies that veterans who fought in the rice paddies, mangrove forests, and jungles of Vietnam were significantly exposed to toxic chemicals. It remains a great mystery how officials at the Veterans Administration and the Department of Defense are so certain that veterans were not exposed to Agent Orange—or that even if they were, that their exposure was insignificant and that their illnesses are unrelated to herbicides. Veterans, in turn, accuse the government of stonewalling and lying.

They are angry, sad, confused, and bitter. Why, they ask, has the nation they served abandoned them? Many will ask this on their deathbeds.

In order to tell their story and to warn people about the dangers of toxic chemicals, Vietnam veterans are willing to appear in courtrooms, on television, or at local and national forums as literal public exhibits. While their lawsuit is on behalf of men, women, and children who are suffering from the effects of Agent Orange, the plaintiffs want their government, and governments throughout the world, to take action to protect future generations from the scourge of toxic chemicals.

But with the settlement, Vietnam veterans and their families never get their day in court.

JUNE 1985

The Brooklyn federal courtroom is packed with reporters, Vietnam veterans and their supporters, lawyers representing the chemical companies, and, oddly enough, beautifully dressed women who seem to be models. Jack Weinstein, the presiding judge, reminds the courtroom that these "fairness hearings" are to ascertain the plaintiffs' reactions to the out-of-court settlement.

Veterans take the stand, some wearing suits, others in combat fatigues or bright orange "Sprayed and Betrayed" tee shirts. They talk about their wives, their deformed children, their friends who are sick and dying, and their fear that Agent Orange will continue to take a heavy toll on their fellow soldiers and their families. Speaker after speaker denounces the settlement as a joke, a fraud, an insult, and yet another example of the government's contempt for its veterans. Some speakers cry. Others break down, unable to complete their testimony.

Squeezed between beautiful women, men with dark suits and fat briefcases actually laugh as veterans testify.

I am sitting with a group of 9th Marines, "the walking dead," who've formed an organization they call the Vietnam Combat Veterans Coalition. The logo on their stationery reads VCVC. Once, I helped them fill a bright orange coffin with copies of *Waiting for an Army to Die* (the coalition calls it their Bible) and other materials on Agent Orange. We wheeled the coffin down the main street in Trenton, New Jersey, and lugged it into the State House. An elderly security guard with a six-shooter hanging on his hip confronted the group, and after a brief discussion he agreed to watch the coffin while we addressed the legislature. We gave extemporaneous speeches to the astonished but friendly representatives and, returning to our coffin, opened the lid and handed out information about Agent Orange to government workers, the press, and to the security guard who allowed us to pass inside.

As laughter continues to fill the courtroom, a VCVC veteran sitting next to me leans over and taps a chuckling man on the shoulder.

"Yes, what is it?" the man demands.

"I want to ask you a question," whispers the marine.

"Question?"

"That's right, a question."

"Yes?"

"Have you ever killed anybody?"

"What are you talking about? What kind of question is that anyway?"

"I said, have you killed anybody?" asks the veteran, leaning until the men's noses are almost touching.

"No, of course not,"

"Well, I have," says the marine. "Now shut the fuck up."

Victor Yannacone, the flamboyant, hot tempered, brilliant lawyer who had filed the Agent Orange class action lawsuit on January 8, 1978, and the only lawyer veterans have ever really trusted, walks to the microphone and begins speaking, but Judge Weinstein cuts him off mid-sentence. Next, it's my turn to speak. But when I start to question the out-of-court settlement, he interrupts me to say that I should go home and run for Congress. That way, he says, I might actually make a real difference.

I wanted to tell him about the morning, May 7, when veterans first heard about the settlement. I answered a call from the wife of a Vietnam veteran living in the midwest. She was pleading with me to talk to her husband. "He's locked and loaded," she said. "And he's on his way to New York City."

"To New York?" I asked. "What is he coming here for?"

"To kill the judge," she said.

She was begging me to talk to a man who'd fought in some of the war's fiercest battles, who said he'd go back to Southeast Asia and fight again if he were asked, a veteran who passionately loved the soldiers with whom he'd served.

I knew this ex-soldier well. His arms and legs were covered with chloracne and his daughter had been born with a serious birth defect.

"Listen, Tommy," I said. "You've suffered enough. You need to think of your kids, your wife, and your fellow veterans. No one wants to see you spend the rest of your life in prison."

A long silence, and I thought he might have hung up or left the house. Then his wife, sobbing with relief, picked up the phone. Her husband, she said, had agreed to put his M-16 back in the closet.

Yale law professor Peter Schuck will one day hail Weinstein as a "genius" for his adroit maneuvering on the Agent Orange class action lawsuit, but in a room packed with ex-soldiers, the presiding judge demonstrates a remarkable naiveté about how the US military and Veterans Administration actually function. When one former paratrooper complains that the VA has treated him with contempt, refusing to acknowledge his illness or treat his symptoms at a local clinic, the judge appears bewildered and shocked.

"But," he replies, shaking his head in disbelief, "the government assures me that they are spending $70 million a year to treat people with Agent Orange problems."

The courtroom bursts into laughter. "With all due respect," says the veteran, "I think you've been lied to."[1]

"Your honor," says the wife of a Vietnam veteran, "I have helped bury lifelong friends who were ripped from their families at twenty-eight years old by an old age cancer. I have watched people I care about in excruciating pain caused by a combination of disorders not to be believed. I have watched good, strong men stripped of their youth, health, jobs, pensions, wives, children, and finally, their identities. I have watched good friends turn their anger on the people who care about them the most. I have held deformed and deathly ill children . . . I found out last week that the wives and children were taken out of this settlement. . . . Is this another strange and mysterious twist in this case?"[2]

Another veteran's wife strides to the front of the courtroom and, shaking with rage, tells Weinstein that she thinks the fairness hearings are nothing but a circus, a sleight of hand designed to trick veterans and their supporters into believing that the judge might reconsider the settlement, perhaps even reject it altogether. The settlement, she says, will be approved;

the chemical companies will continue to make lots of money; lawyers will collect large fees and strut their hour of fame. Meanwhile, Vietnam veterans will continue to bury their brothers in arms. The fairness hearings, says this enraged woman, are a big fraud, an attempt to appease Vietnam veterans and their families, a very bad joke played on victims of Agent Orange.

Five years later, a decision is reached on how the $189 million, ballooned $9 million by interest, will be distributed. The payment plan merely confirms all of the fears and bitterness expressed at the fairness hearings. A totally disabled Vietnam veteran will receive $12,000, but this will be spread out over a period of ten years, and even these meager payments could render the recipients ineligible for supplements like food stamps, public assistance, and government pensions. Widows of Vietnam veterans who can prove their husbands died from Agent Orange exposure will receive $3,700, but the children of Vietnam veterans are entirely excluded.

Meanwhile, the financiers who subsidized the plaintiffs' attorneys receive, as a group, $750,000. An attorney who'd been a "passive investor" will receive $1,700 an hour for his services. One law firm collects over $1.3 million while another receives more than $1.8 million. The court awards a total of more than $13 million in attorneys' fees.[3]

The Vietnam War was not the first time that young men were sent off to kill and die for what their government and their fellow citizens considered a noble cause. Nor was it the first time that young men who'd been sent to war by flag-waving crowds returned home to find that they were expected to keep quiet about the horrors they had seen, were expected to marry, find a job, start a family, and get on with their lives. Men and women who have experienced combat would like to do these things, but they carry scars, memories, and terrors, that will haunt them for the rest of their lives. Vietnam veterans did not want to believe that their government would expose them to chemicals that, years later, would devastate their immune systems, making them susceptible to a host of diseases like kidney failure, heart disease, diabetes, Parkinson's Disease, brain tumors, and various kinds of cancer. They did not want to believe that corporations that profited from manufacturing and selling deadly chemicals would choose to deny their products' toxicity, and that these corporations would refuse to offer to help veterans of what, at the time, was our nation's longest, second most expensive, and most divisive conflict since the Civil War.

Twenty years after the original class action lawsuit is settled out of court, Vietnamese victims of chemical warfare file their own lawsuit, charging the chemical companies with war crimes. By this time, thousands of US veterans have succumbed to the effects of Agent Orange, leaving widows and children to grieve and wonder why the nation chose to ignore the pleas of their loved ones. Lawyers for the Vietnamese plaintiffs believe—with good reason—that they can call on two decades of research to convince a court to rule on behalf of Vietnamese victims of the decade-long defoliation campaign in Southeast Asia. They travel to Vietnam to see at first hand the legacies of chemical warfare in that nation. They study voluminous reports from around the world on the effects of dioxin on animals and human beings, and they consult with Vietnamese doctors and scientists who have devoted their lives to the study of dioxin and to helping victims of Agent Orange. Perhaps most importantly, they visit "peace villages" where they meet children with missing legs and arms, with huge heads, and with scaly burned-bark skin. They build what they believe to be an irrefutable case that will prove, once and for all, that human beings who are exposed to dioxin get sick and die.

The out of court settlement on May 7, 1984, seemed to have ended all hope of securing justice for victims of chemical warfare. But on January 30, 2004, lawyers for the Vietnamese will appear in a Brooklyn federal courtroom to argue their case. The presiding judge will be Jack Weinstein.

CHAPTER 5

A Lucky Man

DANANG, VIETNAM

Nguyen Dinh An has lived through attacks that smashed giant trees into splinters and turned living things to smoking dust. The aircraft that rained bombs upon his unit flew so high that no one could hear them coming. He heard the cries of wounded soldiers, and he watched men die. Low flying planes flew over almost daily, spewing chemicals that killed trees and animals, poisoned the soldiers' food, and made them terribly ill. It was difficult to find safe haven from the bombing raids and impossible to escape the effects of chemical warfare.

For a time during the American War, Mr. An ran a Vietcong propaganda program from the basement of a Marine officers' barracks without being discovered.

Now, Mr. An is Chairman of the Fatherland Front, an organization that is responsible for coordinating charities, NGOs, and other types of organizations in Danang. He is also Chairman of the Danang Union of Friendship Organization.

We thank Chairman An and his staff for meeting with us, and we try our best to display the proper etiquette for this occasion. In Vietnam, you are expected to arrive on time for meetings, properly dressed, and fully prepared not to waste your own or anyone else's time. The Vietnamese workday starts around six a.m. and it ends twelve hours later, with a two-hour midday informal break during which the hustle and bustle of larger towns and cities slows down. Once, I entered a bank during the break to use an ATM. There were no tellers, and the security guard was sleeping on a bench. I felt almost guilty. Another day, forgetting that it was midday break, I walked into a Vietnamese airline (Dragon Air) office, only to find it deserted, except for a woman sleeping on the floor behind the counter. Startled, she was not at all happy to see a sweat-drenched customer.

Our interpreter signals that it is time to start the interview, but my recorder squeaks, stalls, and unravels. A new tape, and Mr. An begins by recalling living in the mountains when planes flew over, dousing the trees with defoliants.

"When the Agent Orange fell," he says, "we took a towel, got it wet and covered our nose, and after that, we went to the waterfall to take a bath. You know cassava? It is like a potato, and it was our major food, but we were told that cassava was very sensitive to Agent Orange, so that's why we tried to chop up all of the cassava we'd planted before.

"So we protected ourselves by taking a bath, and then we chopped all of the cassava. Traditionally, we used green beans, because we believed that green beans would clean up all of the poison from the chemicals. So that's why we cooked green beans with sugar.

"After that we tried to cook all of the cassava, but when it was cooked it had a different color, it turned yellow and tasted different than it had before. But we had to eat that. We knew that the cassava was poisoned, but it was our major source of food and we had no choice but to eat it.

"I don't know how the chemical went into our bodies, but several friends of mine at that time, when we were stationed in the same place, had cancer at a very early age, and they died. The most popular [common] one was liver cancer.

"So I always presume that I am a lucky person. I don't know when my good fortune will be over. I got married after the war ended, and I was very happy with my very first child. She was a normal kid, so I was very happy. Many friends of mine got married after the war ended, they had children, and many of those children had birth defects. So, I had only one child, and didn't want to have a second one because I didn't want to take the chance. We didn't know what it would be like.

"I have seen many families with children, and some of them have birth defects, but others are normal kids. I've seen mental and physical disabilities. In some kids, a part of their face gets a dark complexion. And they have several diseases. Many of them have no arms. There are really a variety of disabilities in Agent Orange kids. Why are some normal? We wonder now if the second generation is affected, and maybe the third generation will also be affected. My experience was very common in Vietnam. Many people experienced Agent Orange in different ways in their life.

"It makes no sense at all that they help the American veterans who served in Vietnam and got affected by Agent Orange, or veterans from New Zealand and Australia, but they totally ignore the Vietnamese people. The American soldiers spent only a short time in Vietnam, in the battlefield, while the Vietnamese people, even those who were fighting for the Saigon regime in the south, spent many years in the war. We appreciate the effort made by the US Congress to help clean up the Danang and Bien Hoa airports. But we also believe that the amount of money needed to help Agent Orange victims must be ten times, or a hundred times greater than the money to clean up these airports."

Nguyen Dinh An believes that one day there will be justice for Agent Orange victims.

"Recently many international lawyers, not just the communist lawyers, but other lawyers in the world showed their support for Vietnamese victims of Agent Orange. We understand that the chemical companies were making a profit from Agent Orange. And sometimes it's hard for people to take responsibility for the mistakes they've made in the past. But the truth is always the truth. More and more people in the world are supporting Vietnamese people."

Mr. An does not agree that Agent Orange is the last obstacle to creating genuine friendship between the United States and Vietnam.

"Many Americans come to Vietnam, visit Agent Orange families, and return home to write articles and make movies like 'Making Peace with Vietnam.' And we do appreciate the efforts that the Americans have been making. We always want to develop our cooperation and friendship with the United States and with the American people. I have many American friends, like Ken Herrmann, who are also veterans in Vietnam. And when we sit together, we always realize that forty years ago we were on two sides of the war. But now we are friends.

"The Danang Union of Friendship Organization, our organization here, is working for this purpose. We want to have a good friendship and be a good partner with the American people. We always welcome US scholars, business men, and NGOs. So we warmly welcome you to Danang, and warmly welcome the effort you have made in writing books about Vietnam."

Listening to Chairman An talk about his exposure to Agent Orange, about seeing men die from the effects of chemical warfare, and about his decision, fearing that his wife might give birth to a deformed baby, to have only one child, I recall hundreds of similar stories from US and Australian veterans. A long time ago, Chairman An might have been trying to kill my fellow countrymen, perhaps even some of my close friends. American and Vietnamese men and women used guns and knives and bombs and booby traps to kill their enemies, and the great irony, if that is the right term here, is that while these soldiers fought ferocious battles, they were all being exposed to the same toxic chemicals. Chairman An lives and works near an area that is still heavily contaminated with TCDD-dioxin, and he understands that even if scientists manage to contain all of the dioxin there, this chemical will continue to harm Vietnamese people for years to come.

If only there had been, years ago, some way to set aside pain and bitterness, recrimination and rage, in order to bring men like Chairman An and US veterans together to talk about the effects of Agent Orange on human beings.

If only popular television hosts had invited Vietnamese and American mothers to talk about giving birth to and trying to take care of deformed Agent Orange children.

If only American scientists had conducted large-scale epidemiological studies on Vietnamese who'd been exposed to Agent Orange/dioxin during the war, and then to compare their findings to studies of American veterans, and veterans from other countries, who served in Southeast Asia.

If only. . . .

Chairman An pins the Danang Friendship medal to my collar.

"Go out to the countryside," he says. "Meet Agent Orange victims. Listen to what these people say. That is the best way to learn about the effects of Agent Orange."

In the morning, Nguyen Thi My Hoa, program coordinator for the SUNY Brockport study abroad program in Danang, will take students to visit Agent Orange families. The students will carry cooking oil, noodles, and other small gifts to poor parents and their seriously handicapped children. These mothers and fathers endure great hardship, but what concerns them the most is how their children will survive once their parents grow too old to care for them, or die. Who will feed them, change their clothing, knead their arms and legs so they will stop screaming in the night? Helpless as newborn rabbits, these children cannot live without constant care from patient, compassionate, loving people.

Chemical warfare has not only damaged the bodies of the children we visit; it has shattered centuries of tradition in which men and women marry young and soon start families, expecting to dedicate their entire lives to their children, knowing that when children grow up, they will fulfill their filial duty to care for their aging parents.

The US military and South Vietnamese military intended to warn people before dousing their fields with toxic chemicals, but in a country lacking basic electricity, telephone service, safe roads, and reliable transportation, it was not possible to do this. Dropping leaflets that people could not read or understand was no help. One minute the planes were overhead, the next they were gone, leaving angry Vietnamese to wonder why the Americans were poisoning the very people whose support they needed in order to win the war.

CHAPTER 6

Generations

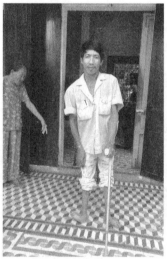

Mr. Dang Van Son

Dang Van Son walks with the help of a metal cane, sliding forward on feet that twist upward at the ankle, like boats swung upright in a storm. His daughter, Dang Thi Hoa, holds on to wooden crutches, her bare feet shaped exactly like those of her father. Mr. Son is forty-two years old. His father fought first against the French for nine years, and then served in the American War for more than a decade. Returning from the jungles after the French surrendered at Dienbienphu, the vet-

eran guerrilla fighter fathered two normal children, a son who
died from disease, and a daughter who is still living. Soon he
was called to war again, living and fighting in mountains that
were saturated with defoliants.

Dang Van Son's father told his family that when he was deep
inside the jungle, the Americans covered the trees with dioxin.
Gagging, gasping for air, and at one point losing consciousness,
he wondered what these strange chemicals the enemy was using
might be. Slowly, his unit made its way to the Ho Chi Minh
Trail, where they tried to recover from their ailments.

When, at last, Mr. Dang's father returned from the fight-

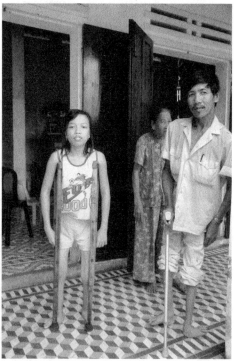

Father and daughter

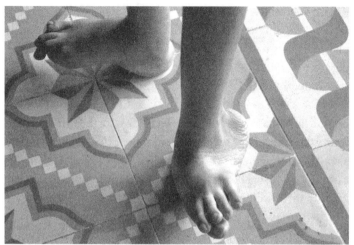

Second generation

ing, he seemed to be healthy and was able to work, even though he suffered from a painful rash and little tumors all over his body. After a few years, he developed throat and stomach cancer, had ulcers "all inside of his stomach," couldn't eat, got "very skinny," and died three months later. He was seventy-six years old.

When the war ended in 1975, soldiers who'd survived the fighting returned to their homes, hoping to spend the rest of their days farming, raising children, and enjoying grandchildren. After decades of war and natural disasters, life was hard in Vietnam. Millions of bombs, landmines, M-79 projectiles, hand grenades, and other unexploded pieces of ordinance were scattered in rice paddies, fields, forests, and waterways. Children picking up cluster bombs lost arms or legs, sometimes their lives. Farmers walking behind water buffalo tripped mines, leaving them crippled for life, or dead.

No one really knew exactly where these deadly weapons were lying, only that if families were to survive, rice must be planted, fields had to be plowed, crops must be harvested. Desperate to earn a living, people lost limbs or died collecting scrap metal to sell. Vietnam was still very much a war zone.

Dang Van Son's father lost track of his fellow soldiers, but he did hear that some of them were in poor health and died soon after returning home. I explain that American veterans are also sick, and many die soon after they reach their late fifties or early sixties. I have heard that only thirty percent of the approximately three million US veterans who served in Vietnam are still alive, though I have no way of verifying that figure.

Mr. Son does not know at what age his father's friends might have gotten ill and died.

Like many Vietnamese, Mr. Son is afraid there will be a third or fourth generation of Agent Orange children. He doesn't doubt that his own and his daughter's deformed (boat) feet are the result of his own father's exposure to herbicides. His daughter, he says, is definitely a victim of chemical warfare.

When asked whether he thinks Agent Orange victims will ever receive compensation for their suffering, he laughs. Yes, he says, he really does hope so. But he can't imagine how that might happen. He worries that his daughter will marry and have an Agent Orange baby. Many Vietnamese parents worry about Agent Orange affecting future generations, but he does not like to dwell on that.

We ask Mr. Son what he might like us to say to President Obama about the effects of Agent Orange on the Vietnamese people, should we ever have the opportunity.

"Please," he says, smiling, "just tell him the truth. Tell him about what you see in Vietnam. What you hear from the Vietnamese people, the Agent Orange victims. Tell him about the suffering. And please ask him to do as much as he can to alleviate the suffering and pain, to help victims overcome the suffering they are feeling every day."

Dang Thi Hoa is a beautiful, intelligent young woman whose handicap should not prevent her from attending school, marrying, and having children of her own. But her family cannot afford a motorbike to carry her to and from school each day, and while she might be able to live near the school, she says she would miss her mother too much.

Mr. Son and his shy young daughter do not complain. They do not ask for pity or demand help for themselves. When one first meets Agent Orange families, this lack of anger might seem odd. Why don't these families blame the United States or the chemical companies for their plight? Why don't they demand compensation—a new house, a motorbike, private medical care? It takes us awhile to understand that the Vietnamese are not merely polite; they are, in fact, a forgiving people.

We promise that if we ever get the chance to speak with President Obama, we will ask him to help victims of chemical warfare. Mr. Son says he watched the Agent Orange Tribunal hearings in Paris in May 2009, on television, and he hopes that those proceedings will help Vietnamese Agent Orange victims.

"I really hope you do talk with Obama," he says.

We offer the family small gifts, take more photographs, and walk into the Vietnam oven. Cows meander along the road, stopping to rest, or munch on something green. A water buffalo stands alone in a rice paddy, waiting for a boy to climb upon his back. Leaving the main highway, we meander down narrow roads and park close to a path leading to a house that is, really, a hut. Baby pigs squeal inside of a bamboo corral. The family's kitchen—a few blackened pans resting upon a wooden stand—is next to the pigs. We leave packages of noodles and a tin of cooking oil, for which the people who live here are very grateful. When the monsoon rains hit, this little camp will be washed away.

China Beach stretches far and away, curving at one point into the sea.

On March 8, 1965, a contingent of US Marines who stormed ashore here were greeted by young Vietnamese women dressed in traditional *aio dai*. The women held up a "Welcome to the Gallant Marines" sign and presented the marines with garlands of flowers.

Except for a scattering of young men drinking beer or napping in lounge chairs, we are alone. A woman brings "Triple 3"—beer, plastic glasses, and a bowl of ice. She is wearing a thick sweatshirt, a scarf wrapped around her face, and long gloves; a strange fashion statement until we realize that Vietnamese women are willing to dress like Eskimos to protect their skin from the sun.

Close your eyes and it's easy to imagine adolescent American warriors frolicking in clear warm water. They are tan, hard-muscled, trained to kill, and—they keep assuring themselves—much too young to die. They play volleyball, chug beer, and count the days until they get to go home.

A short distance from their beach, the streets are teeming with prostitutes, drug dealers, junkies, thieves, Vietcong agents, and black market hustlers peddling weapons paid for by American taxpayers, assembled in American factories, and shipped to Vietnam on American freighters.

Day and night, flocks of aircraft lift off from the runways at Danang's sprawling airbase, some heading to bombing raids, others skimming triple canopy jungles, turning primordial forests into dead zones, leaving behind poisons that will harm Vietnam for generations.

CHAPTER 7

Jurisprudence

In sum, Plaintiffs' suit challenges how the President, with
the support of Congress, chose to prosecute the war in Viet-
nam, and [it] seek[s] reparations that our Nation has
declined to make to the people of Vietnam.

—Attorneys for the defendant chemical companies in
the Vietnamese class-action lawsuit

On January 30, 2004, lawyers representing several million Vietnamese citizens file a lawsuit in a Brooklyn Federal Courtroom,
charging the wartime manufacturers of Agent Orange with war
crimes. Jack Weinstein, the federal judge who handled the 1984
out of court Agent Orange settlement, will preside over and
rule on this new case. In early March 2005, Weinstein dismisses
the lawsuit, writing a 233-page memorandum in which he
attempts to explain why he has chosen, once again, to rule
against the plaintiffs in an Agent Orange lawsuit.

In preliminary hearings, Weinstein tells the plaintiffs'
lawyers:

> I want to emphasize again I have no view about what
> the defendants [Dow Chemical, et al.] knew. I have no
> view as to whether any damage was done. I have no
> view as to whether the law of war or these other inter-

national, human rights laws relied on apply here. But the case has to go forward seriously. We have to address the problems since they are raised. I must say I am dubious at the moment about whether the plaintiffs can make out a case without even getting to the question of causation, but that's based upon my limited reading.[1]

In the mid-1980s, when Vietnam veterans clashed with the manufacturers of Agent Orange, people were still looking for someone to blame for the debacle in Southeast Asia. Treated like pariahs when they returned from Southeast Asia, many veterans hunkered down inside feelings of rage, depression, and alienation, unwilling or unable to talk about their experiences in Vietnam. It was in this context of postwar doldrums that Vietnam veterans started to talk about illnesses they believed were related to their exposure to Agent Orange in Vietnam. Few people wanted to listen, and those who did were skeptical of the veterans' claims that over a period of ten years, the government had exposed its own soldiers to toxic, deadly chemicals.

During the twenty years between the veterans' lawsuit that was settled out of court in 1984 and the Vietnamese class action charging the chemical companies with war crimes:

■ Hundreds of articles about the defoliation campaign in Vietnam, 1961–75, appear in newspapers and magazines in the US, Europe, and other parts of the world.

■ Scientists, doctors, ex-soldiers, Agent Orange advocates, and victims gather at international conferences in Hanoi, Paris, Boston, and Stockholm, to examine the legacies of chemical warfare in Southeast Asia.

■ Filmmakers scour the length and breadth of Vietnam,

documenting evidence of environmental degradation and human suffering related to Agent Orange.

Scientists also release well-researched studies on the effects of Agent Orange/dioxin on human beings. Among them:

■ Researchers conducting a mortality study for the Commonwealth of Massachusetts conclude that "the results suggest that Vietnam veterans may be at increased risk of death due to soft-tissue sarcoma, kidney cancer, suicide, motor vehicle accidents, and stroke compared to non-veterans."[2]

■ A study conducted by the Veterans Administration finds that former Marine Corps ground troops who served in Northern I Corps Region of Vietnam have "died of lung cancer and certain lymph cancers at a significantly higher rate than colleagues who did not serve in the war."[3]

The state of Wisconsin concludes a study of Vietnam veterans, comparing their death rates to Vietnam-era veterans, veterans not of the Vietnam era, and nonveterans within the state of Wisconsin. The study concludes that:

> Relative to other Vietnam-era veterans, those who served in Vietnam had excess mortality from cancer of the pancreas, diseases of the genitourinary system, and pneumonia. An excess of connective tissue cancer was noted when Vietnam veterans were compared with veterans not of the Vietnam era.... No significant excess was noted, however, when Vietnam veterans were compared with other Vietnam-era veterans or with non-veterans.[4]

A West Virginia study concludes:

> Both Vietnam and non-Vietnam veterans experienced
> increased mortality from cancer of the respiratory tract,
> but increases in relative frequency of death from can-
> cer of connective tissues (3 observed vs. 0.7 expected)
> and Hodgkin's disease (5 observed vs. 2.4 expected)
> were confined to Vietnam veterans. When Vietnam
> veterans were compared directly with non-Vietnam
> veterans, these excesses persisted, and, in addition, there
> were more deaths among Vietnam veterans from tes-
> ticular cancer (3 observed vs. 0.6 expected).[5]

An Australian study of 19,205 Vietnam veterans and 25,677
veterans who did not serve in Vietnam determines that:

> In addition to an overall elevated death rate, Vietnam
> veterans had increased death rates for digestive system
> diseases, diseases of the circulatory system, and exter-
> nal causes. The death rates from neo-plasms (all types
> convinced) were similar in the two groups.[6]

1991: Congress passes the Agent Orange Act, entitling veterans who served in the country and who are suffering from
any Agent Orange-associated diseases to health care and disability compensation. In 2009, the Veterans Administration
compensates for a long (and still growing) list of Agent
Orange-related illnesses, including soft tissue sarcoma, chloracne, Hodgkins Disease, multiple myeloma, non-Hodgkin's
lymphoma, diabetes, Parkinson's disease, and prostate cancer.[7]

1994: The Institute of Medicine of the National Academy of
Sciences (IOM) publishes a comprehensive study of the health

effects of exposure to herbicides used in Vietnam, including dioxin. The IOM finds an "association between herbicide exposure and many different types of diseases and defects."[8]

2000: The Environmental Protection Agency states that dioxins, and "in particular the TCDD form contained in Agent Orange are potent and persistent animal toxicants with potential to cause widespread human health effects."[9]

2002: Wayne Dwernychuk of Hatfield Consultants LTD leads a study that finds high levels of dioxin in the soil of the A Luoi Valley and high levels of dioxin in fish, animal fat, human blood, and breast milk.[10]

2003: Dr. Arnold Schecter, professor of Environmental Sciences at the University of Texas, finds that the environment and the food chain in Bien Hoa City are contaminated with dioxin. The study concludes that people continue to be poisoned by dioxin when they eat contaminated food.[11]

In his book-length ruling, Judge Weinstein refuses to accept arguments ("causation") that plaintiffs' injuries—cancer, diabetes, miscarriages, skin rashes, children born with serious birth defects, early deaths—can be traced to their exposure to Agent Orange/dioxin:

> The summary of the harms allegedly caused to plaintiffs or their progeny is set forth by plaintiffs in brief anecdotal form. The fact that diseases were experienced by some people *after* spraying does not suffice to prove general or specific causation, i.e., that the harm resulted to individuals *because* of the spraying. *Post hoc ergo propter hoc* remains a logical fallacy unacceptable in toxic tort law. Proof of causal connection depends primarily upon substantial epidemiological

and other scientific data, particularly since some four million Vietnamese are claimed to have been adversely affected. Anecdotal evidence of the kind charged in the complaint and set out below cannot suffice to prove cause and effect.

Availability of necessary scientific information from Vietnamese studies needed for epidemiological analysis has not been furnished to the court. It is not available with the richness of demographic and other data published in the United States. An agreement between the United States and Vietnam provides for some joint efforts to collect relevant data.[12]

Judge Weinstein writes that US scientists have devised an agreement to collect "relevant data" in Vietnam. He seems unaware that even as preparations for this study appeared to be moving forward, one prominent US scientist, colluding with an employee at the US Embassy in Hanoi, was maneuvering to undermine this project.

At the same time, the US ambassador to Vietnam ridiculed the Vietnamese campaign to help "alleged Agent Orange victims" as "mere propaganda." According to the ambassador, Vietnamese officials were trying to con money out of the United States government. They were also trying to win a propaganda coup.

In a cablegram to the secretary of state, dated February 16, 2003, the ambassador wrote that the government of Vietnam (GVN)

has no intentions of allowing its scientists to engage in genuinely transparent, open, rigorous scientific investigation to determine the true extent of the impact of AO/dioxin on health in Vietnam. Why? Because, we believe, the GVN will never permit research that in any way might discredit the main theme of its two-decade long propaganda campaign, i.e., AO/dioxin is to blame for a huge range of serious health problems—especially birth defects and mental retardation—of residents of central and southern areas and/or northern soldiers who served there.... It would also open a pandors's [sic] box of questions about why the GVN—and more importantly, the Communist Party—has misled its people and focused on demonizing AO/dioxin and failed to carry out appropriate public health programs that would have mitigated other sources of threats to human health.[13]

To the dismay of US and Vietnamese scientists, critics of the cooperative research project managed first to reduce the timeline for the proposed study from five to three years; then, they demanded that the project "be performed only as the US officials required." And finally, they ended all funding for the research, blaming the Vietnamese government for the entire debacle and vowing *never to approve* a *project for US scientists to perform research in Vietnam.*[14]

In one section of his memorandum, "The Harms Allegedly Suffered by Plaintiffs,"

Judge Weinstein writes:

From April 1972 until the end of the Vietnam War in 1975, plaintiff Nguyen Van Guy served in the DRVN [Democratic Republic of Vietnam] army repairing communication lines at various southern Vietnam locations. He ingested food and water from areas that had been sprayed with herbicides. He periodically suffered from headaches, exhaustion and skin irritation while he was stationed in southern Vietnam; the skin irritation disappeared after he left Quang Ngai province in 1973 but the headaches and exhaustion continued, worsening over time. In 1983 his first wife's pregnancy ended in stillbirth. They divorced. His spells of weakness and exhaustion worsened. His second wife, Plaintiff Vu Thi Loan, gave birth to two children, plaintiffs Nguyen Quang Trung and Nguyen Thi Thuy Nga, who were born developmentally disabled. In October 2003, Nguyen Van Guy was diagnosed with stomach cancer and liver damage and found to have fluid in the lung. It is alleged that these diseases conditions and birth defects were caused by his exposure to defendants' [Dow, Monsanto, et al.] herbicides during the Vietnam War.[15]

And:

From 1964 to 1968, plaintiff Dr. Duong Quynh Hoa often traveled to the cities of Bien Hoa and Song Be, which became heavily contaminated with herbicides manufactured by the defendants. From 1968 to 1976, she resided in Tay Ninh province, where she was told several times to cover her head with plastic bags because US aircraft were spraying chemicals. In 1970, she gave birth to a son, Huynh Trug Son. He was born developmentally disabled and suffered from epileptic convulsions; he died from a convulsion at the age of eight months. She had two miscarriages, in July 1971 and January 1972. She was diagnosed with diabetes in

1985 and breast cancer, for which she underwent a mastectomy, in 1998. In 1999, a test revealed relatively high levels of dioxin in her blood. She attributes all these problems to exposure to herbicides manufactured by defendants.[16]

There is page after page detailing miscarriages, skin rashes, cancers, babies living only a few days, babies born with spina bifida, physically and mentally handicapped children, and high levels of dioxin in the blood of fathers and mothers who'd been exposed to Agent Orange/dioxin during and after the war. One typical plaintiff, Ho Xuan Bat, was

active with the NLF in the Aluoi Valley and observed the spraying of herbicides on several occasions. Herbicides were stored, transferred and spilled at several military bases in the Aluoi Valley Region. In 1978, he married plaintiff Ho Thi Le and they continued to live in Aluoi Valley. They cultivated rice and vegetables for their own consumption and to sell in the local market, and consumed wild vegetables, fish and poultry. In 1980, Ho Thi Li gave birth to their first child, who died from a nose infection in 1982. In 1982, she gave birth to their second child, who died for unknown reasons after 16 days. Ho Xuan Bat's health began to deteriorate: he experienced fatigue, headaches, coughing with blood, chest pain, loss of appetite and weight, fever, and other symptoms. In 2003, he was diagnosed with lung cancer and died from it a year later. Ho Thi Le [sic] attributes her miscarriage, the deaths of her two children and her husband's death from lung cancer to their ingestion of

food and water contaminated by herbicides by the
defendants.[17]

The memorandum does not include reference to Dr.
Wilbur McNulty's research in 1982 at the Oregon Regional
Primate Research Center in Portland, Oregon. Dr. McNulty's
research subjects were rhesus monkeys, human beings' nearest
relative (with the exception of chimpanzees) on the evolution-
ary scale. In the beginning, Dr. McNulty put what he thought
were small quantities of dioxin in the monkeys' food. "As fools
rush in," he confided, "the doses, in retrospect, were astronom-
ical. They were in parts per billion instead of parts per trillion
range, which is more relevant when it comes to food. I think
the first level I used was twenty parts per billion in the diet,
and that killed a young male rhesus monkey in twelve days....
A level of 2 parts per billion was lethal in seventy-six days. I
discovered that monkeys are several times more sensitive to
TCDD than mice, rats, rabbits, and dogs."[18]

Dioxin turned out to be so toxic to his laboratory animals
that McNulty decided to suspend all research with TCDD
until the primate center could construct a special building with
carefully controlled access, assigning the care of his monkeys
to only one or two well-trained people in an effort to minimize
the risk of contaminating other areas of the center.

"Dioxin," said McNulty, "is the most toxic small man-made
molecule we know of. It is less toxic on a per-gram basis than
some biological toxins like botulin, but that's a very large molecule. So molecule for molecule dioxin is probably the leader of
the pack."[19]

After consuming food containing minute amounts of
TCDD, McNulty's primates became very quiet, began losing
weight, lost their appetite, grew progressively thinner and

weaker, and then "just laid down and died." Sometimes they would have episodes of retching and vomiting, but at much lower doses of dioxin a certain fraction of animals remained well for one to three or four months, and then suffered from an ailment characterized by failure of the elements of the bone marrow.

"They would have low white blood cell counts, very low platelet counts, so they suffered from hemorrhages and infections and were essentially carried away by bone marrow failure."[20]

McNulty's monkeys did not live in the jungles, mangrove forests, and rice paddies of Southeast Asia for years on end. They didn't eat large quantities of food or drink from rivers and streams contaminated with TCDD-dioxin. They died painful deaths from the toxic effects of a poison that scientists have found to be teratogenic, fetotoxic, carcinogenic, and possibly mutagenic in laboratory animals.

Dioxin is a poison, says Harvard researcher Matthew Meselson, that works on laboratory animals by stopping cell division.

"Spermatogenesis stops, the replacement of red blood cells stops, the regeneration of the epithelial lining of the gut stops. After a few days or weeks without cell division the animals simply fall apart."[21]

Weinstein writes,

It is contended that the acts of defendants adversely affecting plaintiffs constitute violations of the laws and customs of war, also known as war crimes, which prohibit: the employment of poison or poison weapons or other weapons calculated to cause superfluous injury or unnecessary suffering, the wanton destruction of cities, towns, villages or the natural environment, or devastation not justified by military necessity; the use of biological or chemical agents of warfare, whether gaseous, liquid or solid, employed because of their direct toxic effects on people, animals or plants; and the poisoning of food and water supplies in the course of war....

It is alleged that defendants' actions have violated, and plaintiffs' causes of action arise from, the following laws, treaties, conventions and resolutions, which constitute specific examples of the applicable law of nations or customary international law, as well as from domestic national and state laws. [See appendix 1.] Judge Weinstein concludes:

Detailed analysis of international law claims of the Vietnamese plaintiffs establishes that use of herbicides by or on behalf of the United States in Vietnam before 1975 was not in violation of international law.[22]

The United States Senate did not agree to ratify the 1925 Geneva Accords prohibiting the use of poison gases and other forms of biological and chemical warfare until 1975; however, according to Weinstein, even if our government had ratified that treaty, this would not have barred the use of Agent Orange in Vietnam.

The 1925 Geneva Protocol provision was designed to outlaw poison gases such as mustard gas used in World War I. It cannot be interpreted to encompass the use of herbicides which were not then known weapons and were far different in their purpose and effect. The gases outlawed in 1925 had an almost immediate disabling effect on those exposed and were intended to disable or kill human beings. In contrast, herbicides were designed to strip plants of leaves or kill them."[23]

Weinstein argues that if large numbers of people happen to have been poisoned, as a side effect of defoliation in a war zone, that does not constitute a crime against humanity or a violation of any treaty to which the US was a signatory at the time the poisoning occurred. He rejects the Vietnamese plaintiffs' argument that the use of Agent Orange during the war was a violation of international laws prohibiting genocide, enslavement, deportation or forcible transfer of population, torture, or forced pregnancy. Agent Orange and other defoliants were used, he says, to kill trees, not to harm human beings, in Vietnam.

Regarding the government contractor defense—that the chemical companies were only following orders and, therefore can not be sued—Judge Weinstein gives a detailed account of the genocidal use of Zyklon B during World War II. After the war, Bruno Tesch, Joachim Drosihn, and Karl Weinbacher were charged with committing war crimes by supplying poison gas to concentration camps, knowing full well that the gas would be used to kill human beings. Tesch and his partner Stabernow owned a firm that provided technicians—Drosihn was the senior technician—to help carry out gassing operations, and to train the Wehrmacht and S.S. in how to use Zyklon B.

The prosecution in the Zyklon B case argued that the Third Reich had given direct orders to Tesch's firm to supply poisonous gas, and that, fully aware that this product was being used to exterminate vast numbers of people in concentration camps, Tesch and associates followed this order.

The prisoners were charged with violating Article 46 of the Hague Regulations of 1907, which Germany and Great Britain had signed. Tesch claimed that he'd not heard, nor did he know, anything about using Zyklon B to exterminate people in camps like Auschwitz. Tesch's defense team argued that it was one thing to provide a supply of a product meant only to kill human beings, and quite another to sell a product (Zyklon B had been used in small quantities to delouse people) that had other "legitimate" uses.

The prosecution questioned how Tesch and associates could not have known exactly how their product was being used, and that therefore they were guilty of accessories before the fact to murder. Tesch and one associate were found guilty and sentenced to die for their crimes.

In the 1984 class action lawsuit filed on behalf of Vietnam veterans and their families, Weinstein allowed the defendant chemical companies' "government contractor" defense. The companies argued that they told the government what they knew about dioxin, and that they were just trying to help the United States win the war.

Gerson H. Smoger, an attorney who has represented Agent Orange victims for many years, questions the chemical companies' claim that they told the government everything they knew about dioxin.

"I have reviewed literally millions of pages of documents," Smoger told a Vietnamese reporter. "It seems that the manufacturers conspired to hide the dangers from the US government and the rest of the world. The chemical companies knew about the dangers and held secret meetings with the purpose of conspiring to keep the knowledge of the dangers from the US government."[24]

This time, Weinstein denies the government contractor defense, and refuses to accept the argument that the defendants were acting out of necessity when they supplied Agent Orange to the government.

In order to use the Necessity Defense, a defendant must establish:

■ That the criminal conduct of which the defendants stand accused was taken to prevent a greater harm to themselves or others, which was imminent.

■ That there was no effective legal alternative method or course of action available to them that could be taken to avert this so-called harm, and

■ That there was a direct causal relationship between the criminal conduct taken and the avoidance of the alleged harm.[25]

The most serious harm that could have come to defendants if they had refused to supply Agent Orange would have been loss of their manufacturing establishments and other assets through expropriation. Such possible economic harm would not have been more evil than violating international law (*if* it existed), leading to the alleged death and disease of many persons and destruction of much land (*if* there was causation).

We are a nation of free men and women habituated to standing up to government when it exceeds its authority.... Under the circumstances of the present case, necessity is no defense. *If* defendants were ordered to do an act illegal under international law they could have refused to do so, if necessary by abandoning their businesses.[26]

Yet Judge Weinstein denied that lawyers for the plaintiffs demonstrated "causation," and argued that there is no scientific evidence to support the plaintiffs' claims that Vietnamese people are sick and dying as a result of their exposure to toxic herbicides.

Lawyers for the Vietnamese plaintiffs and the chemical company defendants packed their bags, knowing that this was not the last act in the Agent Orange saga. They will meet again in appellate courts, where they will argue before judges who, like Judge Weinstein, will profess compassion and empathy for victims of Agent Orange, but conclude that they can find no way to hold the chemical companies or the government accountable for the legacies of a decade-long campaign of chemical warfare in Southeast Asia.

In one section of his Memorandum, Judge Weinstein deconstructs the international agreements that plaintiffs submit as a basis for their argument that the use of toxic herbicides in Vietnam constituted a war crime.

In response to clause (a) of the 1907 Hague Convention IV, which forbids nations to *employ poison or poisoned weapons:*

> The poisons referenced in clause (a) encompass those applied to specific instruments of warfare such as bullets or bayonets. . . . Even if the terms "Poison" or "poisoned weapons" could be construed more broadly to encompass poisonous gases, this broader definition still would not reach herbicides, regardless of whether they have collateral harmful consequences for humans.[27]

On the subject of war crimes:

> Whoever, whether inside or outside the United States, commits a war crime, in any of the circumstances described in subsection (b) shall be fined under this title or imprisoned for life or any term of years, or both, and if death results to victim, shall also be subject to the penalty of death.

Judge Weinstein writes that:

> Herbicide spraying by the United States did not con-
> stitute "Willful killing" or "willfully causing great
> suffering or serious injury in body or health" since the
> United States lacked the requisite criminal intent.[28]
> The spraying did not constitute "torture" or "inhu-
> man treatment," that is, the defoliation campaign in
> Vietnam did not injure the Vietnamese people's
> human dignity. "As for property damage, any such
> damage was justified by military necessity and was
> carried out lawfully."[29]

On the subject of genocide:

> Genocide: (a) Killing members of the group; (b)
> Causing serious bodily or mental harm to members of
> the group; (c) Deliberately inflicting on the group
> conditions of life calculated to bring about its physi-
> cal destruction in whole or in part; (d) Imposing
> measures intended to prevent births within the group;
> (e) Forcibly transferring children of the group to
> another group.

Judge Weinstein concludes that:

> The United States did not use herbicides in Vietnam
> with the specific intent to destroy any group. Nor were
> those herbicides designed to harm individuals or to
> starve a whole population into submission or death. The
> herbicides were primarily applied to plants in order to
> protect troops against ambush, not to destroy people.[30]

And, in discussing the 1925 Geneva Protocol, which:

> Prohibits the use in war of Asphyxiating Poisonous or
> Other Gases, and of Bacteriological Method of War-
> fare, June 17, 1925.

Judge Weinstein argues that:

> The United States had not signed onto this agree-
> ment. Did sign in 1975. Included a caveat that if an
> "enemy state" or its "allies" fails to respect the Proto-
> col, then the US will no longer be bound by its rules.
> Scholars disagree on what the Geneva Protocol
> means, or does not mean. Unlike the poisonous gases
> outlawed in the Geneva Protocol, herbicides were not
> designed to disable or kill human beings."[31]

Judge Weinstein, a brilliant legal scholar and an honorable
man, ruled against US veterans and Vietnamese victims of
Agent Orange on the basis of what he believed to be objective
interpretations of national and international law. The appellate
courts agreed with his decisions, and on February 27, 2009, the
Supreme Court refused—without comment—to hear arguments on behalf of Vietnamese victims of Agent Orange.

In Vietnam, community workers say they need at least 1,000
new community organizations, known as "Peace Villages"—
currently, they have twelve—to accommodate children who are
suffering from the effects of chemical warfare. Throughout
Vietnam, poverty-stricken parents struggle to take care of
handicapped and seriously deformed children. They do not
express anger, hatred, or blame. Holding boys and girls who

cannot sit up on their own, mothers massage their children's arms and legs, brush their hair, and welcome visitors who are there to offer their support and to witness the effects of toxic chemicals on human beings.

According to lawyers for the chemical companies: "the United States owes no duty in tort to enemy combatants, or even to noncombatants in a war zone. Imposing such a duty on the Government's contractors would undermine the principle, obligating the United States to heed rules of civil conduct that can have no application in the theater of war. ... Entertaining Plaintiffs' challenge to those decisions [military decisions made by the president as commander-in-chief of the armed forces] would risk a stark lack of respect for the Executive Branch and risk multifarious and inconsistent pronouncements by various departments of government."[32]

Furthermore, say the chemical companies, the courts have no right to interfere with the commander-in-chief's decisions during wartime.

No one knows, or will ever know, exactly how many American and Vietnamese citizens have died from exposure to dioxin since Victor Yannacone filed the Agent Orange product liability class action lawsuit in 1978. There is no count of the number of miscarriages and stillbirths Vietnamese and American women married to veterans have experienced in the past thirty-five years. The United States has no idea how many American children born with serious birth defects have fathers or mothers who served in Vietnam. No one will ever know how many American, Korean, Australian, New Zealand, and Vietnamese veterans have died from cancer and other Agent Orange related diseases since the war ended.

The Agent Orange tragedy has become a rather elaborate game of "you get your lawyer, I'll get mine," and "You get your scientist, I'll get mine." I'm not suggesting that all of the actors in this decades-long drama are nefarious characters or indifferent to human suffering. But I have to wonder what Thomas Jefferson and other founding fathers might have to say about the chemical companies' arguments that the United States of America does not have to "heed the rules of civil conduct that can have no application in the theater of war."

That the United States "owes no duty in tort to enemy combatants or even to noncombatants in a war zone."

That the plaintiffs in the Vietnamese class action suit must not be allowed to question military decisions "made by the President as commander-in-chief of the armed forces."

And that the courts have no right to interfere with decisions the commander-in-chief makes in wartime.

Does this mean that the president can initiate a campaign to bomb another nation, as Lyndon Baines Johnson did in 1964, based upon fabrications and lies? Can the United States attack another nation, using chemical weapons against its environment and its people for years, without being held responsible for maiming, starving, and killing noncombatants? Would questioning the commander-in-chief's right to make military decisions that will result in the deaths of millions of innocent civilians indicate a lack of respect for the executive branch?

Lawyers for the chemical companies seem to be saying that when the president is acting as the commander-in-chief, he turns into a king. Would Jefferson agree?

CHAPTER 8

The Last Family

*Occasionally I saw these [genetically deformed] children in
contaminated villages in the Mekong Delta; and whenever
I asked about them, people pointed to the sky; one man
scratched in the dust a good likeness of a bulbous C-130
aircraft, spraying.*

—John Pilger

On the outskirts of the city of Danang, women in conical hats
tend rice paddies, bending in calf-deep water to plant new
shoots. Brown cows and steel-gray water buffalo graze this
ancient landscape, at peace now after centuries of invasions,
uprisings, and war. We cross a narrow bridge, turn into a dirt
road, and walk a short distance to a small, remarkably barren
house, its walls scarred by monsoon flooding, and only the
most rudimentary furniture—a low glass-covered wooden
table, small red plastic chairs, no television or family shrine. It
is the kind of home that one might find in the most destitute
areas of Appalachia or on impoverished Indian reservations.

Nguyen Thi May sits on the floor, a twelve-year-old boy
sprawled on her lap; her sixteen-year-old daughter, Trinh, leans
close by her side. Until a recent operation on her legs, paid for
by World Vision Vietnam, Trinh could not walk; now, her
mother explains, she can move about "a little." The girl's skin is

Nguyen Thi May and her children

wrinkled and dry, like bark that might just peel away when touched, or catch fire in the Vietnam heat—we would later see a boy with this same condition, called x-linked ichthyosis, at a hospital in Ho Chi Minh City. When her mother bathes her, Trinh's skin peels off, turns white, and then darkens like red wine. Trinh will never attend school or learn to care for herself, and while she smiles and waves one hand at her visitors, most of the time she stares about the room, expressionless.

Nguyen Thi May's husband, Pham Xong, confides that his son's head is growing larger, while the boy's body remains the same. Twelve-year-old Phan Van Truc suffers from seizures, and his parents say they never know when they might occur. He cannot speak or walk, he requires constant attention, and he will never get any better. His father worries that the boy appears to be getting weaker, a condition that defies explanation.

The children seem happy to see students from SUNY Brockport's study abroad program, and when Brendan takes photographs of the boy sitting on his father's lap, he grins and wiggles his feet. Pham Xong and Nguyen Thi May do not own a motorbike, and they move their children about on a rough-hewn wooden cart. One parent must be at home at all times, making it difficult for the family to earn money. Doctors have examined these children and determined that their birth defects are symptomatic of exposure to dioxin, but there are no funds available to examine the father's sperm, blood, or fatty tissue. Pham Xong is forty-seven years old; his wife is forty-two, young enough, when their children were conceived, to have given birth to healthy offspring.

Some years after the last official American spray mission in the Central Highlands, the children's father served with the

Father and son

army in that region. He recalls once when many men in his unit began choking, and became so ill that they had to be medivaced to a hospital. Pham Xong also served in Cambodia, close to the border of Vietnam, an area that was heavily sprayed with defoliants. Skeptics might argue that most of the dioxin in these regions had probably washed out of the soil; however, this does not take into account the fact that the half-life of dioxin on surface soil fluctuates between nine and twenty-five years, and in deeper levels from twenty-five to one hundred years.

According to Dr. Alan Schecter, one of the world's experts on dioxin, "a person may be found with dioxin in his/her blood after 35 years of getting contaminated."[1]

Thirty-five years after the last spray mission in Vietnam, scientists have found astonishing levels—up to 1,000 times the permissible level in the United States—of dioxin at former military bases like Bien Hoa, Danang. There are no reliable studies of how many people living near these bases may have been heavily exposed to dioxin, or what the future consequences for these people and their offspring might be. It is clear that dioxin has entered the food supply of people who live near bases from which the Air Force flew thousands of defoliation missions.

In 1967, Arthur W. Galston, a renowned professor of Botany at Yale University, tried to warn the US against the continued, unbridled use of herbicides in Vietnam:

"We are too ignorant of the interplay of forces in ecological problems to know how far-reaching and how lasting will be the changes in ecology brought about by the widespread spraying of herbicides. The changes may include immediate harm to people in sprayed areas."[2]

Galston's warning turned out to be prophetic. Just two years later, reports of birth defects in the offspring of Vietnamese women began to appear in Saigon newspapers.

At the New York Temporary Commission on Dioxin Exposure hearings in 1981, a Vietnam veteran testified that "before my son was ten and a half months old, he had to have two operations because he had bilateral inguinal hernia, which means his scrotum didn't close, and his intestine was where his scrotum was, and his scrotum was the size of a grapefruit. He also has deformed feet . . . My oldest daughter has a heart murmur and a bad heart. Once she becomes active, you can see her heart beat through her chest as though the chest cavity is not even there, as though you were looking at the heart."[3]

At the same hearings, a Vietnam veteran's wife testified that she was married to a Vietnam veteran who was in combat in 1967 and 1968.

"We have two sons," she said, "a four-year-old and one who is four months. Our first son was born with his bladder on the outside of the body, a sprung pelvis, a double hernia, a split penis, and perforated anus.

"We have met other veterans," she continued, "and their families. We have met their children. We have seen and heard about the deformities, limb and bone deformities, heart defects, dwarfism, and other diseases for which there is no diagnosis. . . . There are hundreds of children with basically the same problem, but in groups; so many bifidas, so many bone deformities, urological, neurological. But it is in groups of hundreds, not ones or twos."[4]

In a study, "Genetic Damage In New Zealand Vietnam War Veterans," Louise Edwards writes:

> Tuyet and Johansson (2001) conducted a study on Vietnamese women and their husbands who were

exposed to Agent Orange during the Vietnam War. The authors found that 66 percent of all children had some type of major health problem. Thirty-seven percent of these children were born with some visible malformation or disability while 27 percent had developed a disability during the first year of life. Of the 60 children suffering from health problems, 40 were unable to attend school but were able to help with agricultural work and domestic chores. Twenty children were disabled very severely physically and mentally, and required 24-hour care needing to be attended to by their parents for every need. There were no cases of congenital malformation nor other disabilities among unexposed siblings of the husbands and wives, nor among the children of their siblings.[5]

Addressing the concerns of New Zealand veterans who worried about the effects of Agent Orange/dioxin on their own children and future generations, the report stated:

The results from the SCE study show a highly significant difference between the mean of the experimental group and the mean of the control group (p < 0.001.) This result suggests, within the strictures of interpreting the SCE assay, that this particular group of New Zealand Vietnam War veterans has been exposed to a harmful substance(s) which can cause genetic damage. Comparison with a matched control group would suggest that this can be attributed to their service in Vietnam. The result is strong and indicates that further scientific research on New Zealand Vietnam veterans is required.[6.]

Pham Xong and his wife realized early on that their daughter was suffering from serious birth defects; however, they hoped to have at least one child who could live a normal life and help them in their old age. Instead, their son could neither walk nor talk, had seizures, and would never outgrow his handicaps. That's when they decided not to have any more children. They are aware that there is no cure for dioxin exposure, yet they do not blame anyone for their plight.

Preparing to leave, I hesitate, trying to think of something we might do to ease this family's burden. It's difficult to say goodbye to families like this one. We walk into their barren little houses, produce a tape recorder, and ask painful questions. Then, we take photographs, and we leave an envelope containing 100,000 Dong, the equivalent of about $12, for which the recipients are genuinely grateful.

I could apologize for our government's indifference to the plight of Agent Orange victims, but that feels rather self-indulgent, and might embarrass this gentle family. I could promise to return with a shaman who will give their son the power of speech and their daughter the ability to walk, but I don't know anyone who possesses powers like that. The families we visit will never sit in an air-conditioned theater, munching buttered popcorn while beautiful actors make them feel happy and frightened and safe and wonderfully sad. They won't join friends in a cheerful restaurant, drinking wine and eating until they're pleasantly stuffed. Their children will not spend hours talking on a cell phone, planning weekend parties, being young and strong and full of optimism.

All we can do is promise that we will tell people about the extraordinary families we meet, the beautiful children, the determination, the courage, and the terrible suffering we encounter in Vietnam. We must hope, as the Vietnamese do, that this will be the last generation of children to suffer from the effects of chemical warfare.

Pham Xong and his wife pose with their children for photographs as a loving family, which they most certainly are.

During the monsoon rains last year, water poured into this tiny house, climbing so high (water marks on their green walls) that the family was in peril of drowning. A charitable organization will build the family a balcony, so that when the rains flood their living room this year, they won't die.

CHAPTER 9

The Realm

A myth has been created by the chemical companies that the
US government somehow designed Agent Orange and that
this was a special, unique chemical. IS NOT TRUE.

—Gerson Smoger, J.D, PhD

JUNE 2007, MANHATTAN FEDERAL COURT

An attorney representing Dow Chemical Company is speaking before a panel of three appellate court judges, trying to convince them that the Vietnamese class action lawsuit charging Dow and three dozen wartime manufacturers of Agent Orange with war crimes is without merit, and that the court should dismiss plaintiffs' appeal post haste.

Among spectators in the packed courtroom is fifty-one-year old Nguyen Van Guy, who is suffering from terminal cancer, and has two children with birth defects. Speaking outside of the courtroom, he tells spectators and the press: "I am here as living evidence to tell the people in the court that dioxin really has a negative impact on human beings as well as the environment."

Mr. Guy has come to America to seek justice.

"The chemical companies," he says, "must be forced to pay compensation to me and my children."

Soon after he returns to Vietnam, Mr. Nguyen Van Guy will die from his wartime exposure to Agent Orange.

Nguyen Thi Hong is also in the courtroom. Exposed to Agent Orange during the war, and afterward while living near Bien Hoa, a dioxin "hot spot," Ms. Hong suffers from multiple cancers, liver problems, and other illnesses. She is sixty years old. One month after returning home to Vietnam, she too dies.

Vo Thanh Hai did not participate in the war, but soon after the fighting ended he moved his family to Nam Dong province, where they helped replant trees in defoliated areas. "My mission," says Mr. Hai, "was to rebuild the country after so many years of war. That is why my family did not hesitate to move in a region we knew was a hot spot for Agent Orange."[1]

These plaintiffs are aware that they may not live to see the wartime manufacturers of Agent Orange accept responsibility for their actions. Nevertheless, they are here to represent impoverished Vietnamese victims of Agent Orange, their children, and all of those who have died and who will die in Vietnam and other parts of the world from exposure to dioxin.

Court adjourns for lunch and a crowd gathers in Foley Square for an impromptu rally. At one end of the plaza, about fifty angry demonstrators wave the Republic of South Vietnam flag—three red stripes over a yellow background. They hold banners scrawled with anti-communist slogans, and shout at people they appear to consider traitors—including American veterans who are here to express their support for the Vietnamese people.

It isn't clear why these demonstrators are here, or what is making them so angry. A woman approaches the demonstrators. She shouts in Vietnamese; they shout back and strike at her with a flagpole. It seems that the enraged group thinks

Agent Orange is a communist conspiracy. The press ignores the enraged demonstrators, and the police take no action when a man tries to smash a pole over a woman's head.

We return to the courtroom.

When the chemical companies' lawyers are speaking, the judges are convivial, friendly, and prepared to laugh; when lawyers representing the Vietnamese address the court, the panel seems irritable, confrontational, and impatient. But why wouldn't these judges be irascible? Day after day, week after week, year after year, this drama unfolds with morose predictability. If feels like a drama in which everyone—audience, actors, directors—knows the script by heart, and yet, motivated by hope that one day there will be something new, they keep on coming. Years pass, then decades. Players come and go. Now and again, someone might try to improvise, giving the drama new energy, creating the possibility of a surprising outcome. But the producers and directors of this theater adhere to an absolute and inflexible set of rules. The script cannot be revised, even when, exhausted, the audience gives up and goes home.

The three appellate judges do not ask the Vietnamese plaintiffs who've traveled 10,000 miles to this hearing if they'd like to address the court. They do not ask them why they might be willing to spend their last days making up stories about the effects of Agent Orange on their children, their friends and neighbors, themselves. Would the panel like to see photographs of Mr. Guy's children, examine doctors' reports on Ms. Hong's illnesses, or invite Vietnam veterans in the courtroom to talk about their experiences with Agent Orange? Spectators are not allowed to suggest ways to energize this dull drama. The afternoon drones on.

At lunch, the veteran sitting next to me talked about humping through dark triple-canopy jungles screaming with life; then suddenly the ground was carpeted with dead birds and monkeys and all he could hear was the sound of frightened men hoping to survive another search and destroy mission.

"This is bullshit," he grumbles, getting to his feet. "I was there. They"—he points to the judges—"weren't."

Federal marshals watch him move slowly down the aisle and out the door. The man from Dow shuffles papers, clears his throat, and speaks. "According to Sosa," he says. The panel nods.

Spectators retrieve their cell phones and other belongings. Elevator doors open and close, and reporters talk to exhausted Vietnamese who've spent the entire day in the courtroom.

In Manhattan federal court, dying Vietnamese plaintiffs and their supporters stood up to the chemical companies and the US government. No one expects the court to rule in favor of the Vietnamese. Twenty years ago, the chemical companies prevailed over a team of prominent lawyers representing Vietnam veterans and their families. The stakes are higher now. If the chemical companies lose, they might have to pay billions in compensation, rather than the $180 million they agreed to award US veterans. If the chemical companies win, they will most likely declare the long-standing conflict over Agent Orange to be finally over.

On the subway later that day, the train stops every two minutes, but that's okay because it gives me time to ponder the realm of law. Entering this world is a walk through Alice's Wonderland, where one hears all sorts of strange, contradictory, and confusing conversation. But ordinary people, not rabbits and caterpillars, argue cases before judges in quite ordinary courtrooms. Human beings, not Cheshire cats, listen to arguments, rule on the case before them, and write legal briefs explaining why they chose to decide the case one way or the other. Still, it can be disconcerting when erudite people speak and write in a language that *feels* the way a stone might sound if it could talk.

It's easy to get confused, bewildered, and even lost inside of the Realm of Law. Translating circumlocution into readable prose might help, but that would require lots of time and patience.

> THE COURT: This case involves international human rights issues of great significance to the country, the plaintiffs and to others in the international field and it has got to be decided ... I want to make it clear to everybody that at the end of six months, I want to have a decision by this court that can go to the Court of Appeals on all the issues that can be decided pre-liminarily, except the issue of whether the Agent Orange, in fact, causes the diseases and other problems alleged.... I do not want discovery on allegations of poisoning of Vietnamese land or poisoning water and so on as a fact.[2]

What you assumed the speaker or writer might be saying requires new interpretations, new translations. Words thump across the room or page, stand upon their head, perform cart-wheels and somersaults. It's time for coffee, a walk with the dog, a little poetry.

After a nice break, you return to the task at hand, refreshed, prepared to unravel double negatives, murky phrasing, and sentences that move forward, only to switch back again and again, like perilous mountain roads:

MR. BROCK [lawyer for a defendant company]: We are making a fine distinction because Your Honor has asked us not to go into the question of causation, and yet, to respond to a claim that we knew that the spraying was going to cause harm. I think there is a distinction as to the historical fact and to what would have been known at the time, but I think, you know, the fact that it remains uncertain at best and in fact, it seems unsupported 40 years later after intensive scientific investigation is a pretty important consideration, and realizing people cannot have possibly known that the contrary was the case 40 years ago.

THE COURT: Well, that is a subtle point. It is an accurate point, I will take it into account.[3]

The plaintiffs cannot establish that a binding international norm "prohibited private corporations from manufacturing and selling herbicides for military use":

Even if forgoing instruments had created a binding prohibition on the use of herbicides during war prior to 1975—and they manifestly did not—they created no universally recognized prohibition on the manufacture and sale by private parties of herbicides intended for such use. Indeed, the general rule is that international legal norms impose duties or confer rights directly upon an individual human being.[4]

We sit outside on a small terrace behind the kitchen. Trinh Kokkoris serves coffee and there's a pastry from a local shop. It is a hot day in July. Planes lifting off from JFK International swallow our words. We wait until the noise fades, then continue our conversation.

Dean Kokkoris has been working on the Vietnamese class action lawsuit for many years, and he's invited me to his home to talk about this case.

Dean grew up in Bayside, Queens, where his father owned a series of Greek restaurants. He attended Baruch College, City University of New York, intending to major in business, but, he laughs, "I changed [my father's] mind after the very first class. Switched to psychology, and met Trinh. We were in *Guys and Dolls* together, she as a Hot Box Girl, and I played Rusty Charlie in a fedora hat and a pinstriped double-breasted suit."

After graduation, Dean found a job as a paralegal at a big law firm, took the test to become a New York City police officer, and passed in the top ten percent of applicants. His parents and wife encouraged him to take the law school exam; he did, then turned down a scholarship offer from Brooklyn Law School.

"I was scheduled to take the police department's psychological exam. Might not have passed that one. Why not go ahead and be a policeman? Retire after twenty years at half salary. But I decided to attend law school, was re-offered the scholarship, earned my degree, and kind of drifted, working as a summer associate at a midsize firm that represented a lot of companies like Amtrak, some municipalities. They liked me and extended an offer, but I wanted to work in the District Attorney's office. Applied to all five boroughs, even to people I knew, but didn't have any political connections."

Dean opened a "kind of blue collar law firm with a friend," and got involved with lawyers who practice labor law—wage and hour law, minimum wage, overtime, prevailing wage. "Workers who aren't getting paid enough for what they do."

Trinh fills the pastry dish and pours more coffee. Born in

Saigon at the height of the defoliation campaign, she was seven years old when her family immigrated to the United States in 1975. She suffers from a lot of allergies, unusual in her family, and Dean wonders if her ailments have anything to do with Agent Orange. He knows that the US military sprayed Agent Orange close to Saigon, but thinks that Saigon might have been spared, even though the Rach Son stream in Cu Chi district feeds into the Saigon River, and food supplies coming into the city were probably contaminated with dioxin.

At one point in his career, Dean became quite interested in cases that the Center for Constitutional Rights was pursuing, using the Alien Torts Claims Act (ATCA).

"They'd brought a case against a military commander in Peru who was torturing people. In the 1990s, the Center also brought a series of cases against corporations using the ATCA, which allows individuals to sue corporations or persons for violations of international law. For example, grievous violations of international law, like the Center's case against UNICAL on behalf of people living in Myanmar, or Burma. UNICAL entered into a joint venture with the Burmese military to build a gas pipeline, and they were using forced labor to construct this pipeline. They were drafting people from local villages that the pipeline was passing through and forcing them to work on this project, which is a violation of international law."

Dean followed the case against Royal Dutch Shell, when the Center was trying to get that company to stop drilling in sacred Oragoni land in Nigeria. Royal Dutch Shell was accused of collaborating with the Nigerian military in the murder of Oragoni people.

"Then I saw a notice in the *National Lawyers Guild* asking if anyone was interested in bringing a case on behalf of Vietnamese who'd been exposed to dioxin, and when I saw that, I jumped."

Dean had been on the *Law Review* at Brooklyn Law School, researching and writing about Bendictin, a pill that was developed for morning sickness. The FDA had approved Bendictin, and women who were taking it claimed that it caused birth defects. Dean was familiar with statistical techniques for determining cause, which is difficult to do, he realized, because the government and corporations do not test chemicals on human beings.

"So the thing is with these drugs or chemicals that may cause birth defects, miscarriages, cancer, is that the scientific causes are not known in the same way that scientists understand, say, infections.

"We test chemicals on animals, but you cannot necessarily extrapolate from animals to humans. Ideally what you'd want to do—you really wouldn't want to do this—is conduct experimental studies with human beings. You'd have two groups: A control group and an experimental group. Give the drug to an experimental group and a placebo to the control group and see what happens.

"Of course we don't do that. We wait until someone is exposed to a chemical or takes a pill, and then we find a similar group of people who have not taken this pill, or who haven't been exposed to this chemical. We take into consideration other environmental factors in their lives—smoking, drinking, and exposure to toxic chemicals. And then we run statistical tests. The larger the group, the more power your study will have, and the more accurate your study will be, with a chance for a statistically significant difference between the group that was exposed and the one that was not.

"In the case of dioxin, with many people in different circumstances, you can see a 'spike.' Think about it. Veterans came back from the war in Vietnam, not knowing where guys in their unit might live. In many cases, they lost contact altogether with their fellow soldiers, but later these veterans from all over the country and the world begin to have similar problems—cancers, birth defects, and other illnesses. A veteran living in Montana could not have known about the problems a vet in New York or California is experiencing. Yet their stories are remarkably similar."

Dean talks about the difficulties of conducting scientific tests that might prove causation. It's really not possible to create ideal conditions, studies take many years, and like the tobacco companies who claimed for so many years that there was no real proof that smoking harms human beings, the chemical companies use similar arguments when they insist there's no evidence that dioxin harms human beings.

"I had a better understanding than most people of what it means when a scientist advocating for the chemical companies says, 'Well, Dean, you can't prove that dioxin causes anything.' All that means is that no one has spent the time and money to do the requisite studies in Vietnam that are required to prove causation. Why haven't the chemical companies or the US government done these kinds of studies? Certainly the American government doesn't have the incentive. And the companies that manufactured Agent Orange don't have the incentive.

"So the only place where you have the kind of mass exposure to dioxin that you could do a meaningful study with enough people, where you could do a high-powered study, would be in Vietnam."

The Vietnamese have conducted scientific studies; however, some American scientists refuse to accept this research.

"In those scientists' minds, the Vietnamese standards don't rise to the 'acceptable level of Western standards.' And I put that in quotes."

"Scientific research," says Dean, "leaves little doubt that dioxin harms animals and human beings. Dioxin is a known carcinogen, and in terms of the other things—birth defects, miscarriages, and other illnesses—it is well established that dioxin causes these things in animals.

"I mean, you start to examine what effect this substance, dioxin, has on the human cell. And then you move on by feeding it to animals, and scientists have learned that dioxin interferes with the reproductive system, it causes birth defects, and it causes miscarriages and all kinds of cancers and tumors. So there's a lot of evidence there.

"The chemical companies benefit from *not* doing the studies. That way, they can say that there is *no evidence* that dioxin harms human beings. After all, if they did the kind of studies I'm talking about, they might actually prove that what American, Korean, Australian veterans, New Zealand, the Vietnamese, and others are saying about dioxin is true."

Dr. Wayne Dwernychuk, a senior Canadian scientist who worked the with Hatfield Consultants to locate the most contaminated areas in Vietnam, thinks there's no need for more studies to prove that Vietnamese exposed to Agent Orange are in danger.

"My point has always been," says Dwernychuk, "that the toxicity and potential health issues related to dioxin are not really disputed. . . . With this as a firm background, removing the exposure potential for hundreds of thousands of Vietnamese to dioxin contaminated lands/food/sediments should be the primary goal. . . . If there are enough funds, which I can almost guarantee there won't be, health studies on the Vietnamese population could proceed."[5]

The humidity is rising and the noise from JFK International makes it difficult to hear. We have to stop mid-sentence and wait for aircraft to gain altitude. Trinh suggests we move inside where it's cool and quiet.

"It's important," Dean continues, "to remember that the wartime manufacturers of herbicides for use in Vietnam never intended to manufacture dioxin. They would not have wanted to do that. But at some point they did realize that dioxin is a byproduct of baking trichlorophenol, which is a component of 2,4,5-T, one half of Agent Orange. The chemical reaction to make trichlorophenol happens in an autoclave, which is something like an oven. It's a machine that heats up this stuff. I guess you could say it cooks it. A couple of German researchers working for C. H. Boehringer Sohn Company back in the fifties published an article in a scientific journal identifying dioxin as being responsible for chloracne, a serious skin rash from which people who've been exposed to this chemical often suffer.

"C.H. Boehringer Sohn discovered a way to minimize the dioxin content in a substance by keeping down the temperature in the autoclave. Dow purchased this information from Boehringer Sohn, and the company knew how to reduce levels of dioxin when it started making Agent Orange in the early sixties.

"Dow, Monsanto, and Diamond Shamrock were able to make a batch of Agent Orange in about forty-five minutes, but if they'd lowered the temperatures, it would have taken a lot longer—possibly twelve hours—to make the same batch of herbicide. By keeping the autoclave temperatures higher, they made it more quickly and for a lot cheaper. Dow and other manufacturers of Agent Orange ignored the safety precautions because they wanted to make Agent Orange more quickly, and they wanted to make more of it."

We pause for lunch and more coffee. It is Saturday. Dean might prefer to spend it puttering around the house, going to the beach, or relaxing with a good book in his comfortable living room. Dean has been giving talks on college campuses to students who want to learn about the Vietnam War. He tells them about Agent Orange, how once the defoliation campaign started, it kept expanding, covering more land, killing more trees, more food, and no one knew how to stop it. He understands that students might find it hard to believe that corporations were willing to profit from manufacturing and selling millions of gallons of deadly chemicals. Dean speaks in a soft, deliberate voice. He does not exaggerate or embellish. He doesn't have to. Like any good horror story, this one tells itself.

According to the defendants' lawyers, those living in a warzone, or who just happen to *be* in one when fighting erupts, have no recourse to the law:

> The Supreme Court has recognized for more than a century that no civil liability attaches to personal injuries sustained or property damages arising from combatant activities during war. To the contrary, the Court has made clear that "[t]he destruction or injury of property in battle, or in the bombardment of cities and towns, and in many other ways in the war, ha[s]to be borne by the sufferers alone as one of its consequences. . . ." As the Court of Appeals explained in *Koohi*, "it simply does not matter for purposes of the 'time of war' exception whether the military makes or executes its decisions carefully or negligently, properly or improperly. It is the nature of the act and not the manner of its performance that counts."[6]

"There's no dispute that the chemical companies knew about dioxin and did not tell the government what they knew while they were supplying it," Dean explains. "But the argument Weinstein patched together is unconvincing. By the way, I took a class from Weinstein when I was in law school, on scientific evidence.

"Judge Weinstein claimed that the government knew just as much as the chemical companies about the dangers of dioxin because, he said, the US was going to build its own herbicide plant at Wellman Springs. Moreover, even before the defoliation campaign began in Vietnam, scientists at chemical weapons labs had adjoining offices with other government agencies that studied the effects of dioxin on cancer.

"Weinstein creates this very broad definition of government. The fact is that the US military *knew nothing about the presence of dioxin in Agent Orange.* Nor did the procurement people who purchased herbicides from the chemical companies know anything about dioxin. Nevertheless, Weinstein stretches his argument so far as to say that scientists at various regulatory agencies, not really connected with the use of Agent Orange in Vietnam, knew about dioxin.

"He extrapolated from what scientists in individual agencies *might have known* to what the government, as an entity, *had to have known.*

"So the latest court of appeals panel had to be much more careful how they approached this case. 'Okay,' they told us, ' you know what? We have evidence here that we did not have before in the last round of appeals. And you guys actually made a very good case for the chemical companies *knowing* about the dangers of dioxin, and not telling the government about that.'"

The Court realized that the companies clearly knew there were scientific methods for reducing the content of dioxin in Agent Orange that they did not pass on to the government. But that was not enough to sustain the plaintiffs' appeal. Because, said the Court, even if the defendants had disclosed this information to the government, it wouldn't have made any difference; the government was going to use defoliants in Vietnam anyway.

"Now, what the court is actually doing here is reading into the *intent* of the military command and the government procurement people."

This argument, Dean explains, is disingenuous because the minute Ralph Nader's raiders leaked the study that Bionectics labs conducted for the National Cancer Institute—the results of this study had been kept under wraps—the military ended the Ranch Hand missions in Vietnam and, soon, issued orders to stop using Agent Orange.

"For the court of appeals to say that the government would have continued defoliation missions, even if it knew the dangers of dioxin, is nonsense."

Dow and other companies did have superior information, and they did not pass it on to the government. Dow found out about dioxin when employees developed chloracne, an indisputable symptom of dioxin exposure, after workplace accidents. Dow even stopped production in one of its facilities, contacted this German company that had experience with dioxin, and called a meeting in March 1965 in Midland, Michigan.

"They called in representatives of all of the companies— Monsanto was not present, but did correspond with Dow about this—that were supplying Agent Orange at that time. And they said: 'Look, we've discovered this stuff called dioxin in our product. It's not intentional, but it's there.' And Dow said it knew about some of the effects of this chemical. The company knew that dioxin causes chloracne, and that dioxin is conceivably a potent carcinogen. There was already evidence that dioxin causes liver damage, and *porphyria cutanea tarda*. It's systemic and toxic to the system. Dow knew all this, and the company was worried that if the government found out, it would step in and regulate the manufacturers. They'd lose a lot of money. So, said Dow, 'Let's just keep this to ourselves.'"

"Agent Orange was twenty-five times more concentrated than domestic 2,4,5-T.

No doubt that Dow made a deliberate attempt not to communicate all it knew about dioxin to other manufacturers."

Dean points to a meeting at the Army's Edgewood Arsenal to evaluate the safety of Agent Orange and its effects on humans and animals, a meeting at which the chemical companies failed to report their own workplace incidents. Agent Orange, they said, was harmless to humans and animals. Later, commanders in the field, not knowing any better, assured soldiers that defoliants were safe.

"Clearly, those companies were not forthcoming with what they knew about dioxin. And it's important to note that chemical companies do not assert in court that they told the government what they knew about Agent Orange.

"Their argument is simply that the government knew about dioxin. And they argue that what they knew is insignificant because it doesn't approach the level of proving causation. Companies continue to argue that there is no proof that dioxin causes illness, even cancer. They argue that if you can't prove causation now, forty years after the war, how could you expect us to have known about it, or to have told anyone about it, back then?

"The chemical companies concede that there might have been a few minor complaints about Agent Orange, and a few insignificant incidents in the workplace over the years, but it's nothing to worry about. After all, there's no sound medical proof that dioxin harms human beings, which is why they say they didn't report these minor problems.

"At the meeting in 1965, Dow announced that the company has a gas chromatography machine. The lowest amount of dioxin this machine can detect in 2,4,5-T is 1 part per million (ppm). Since that was the lowest level their scientists could detect, Dow concluded that this must be a safe level. During the war, none of the manufacturers kept dioxin down to that level. There were measures of dioxin up to 40 to 50 ppm, even 140 ppm. Dr. Jean Stellman, a researcher at Columbia University, estimated the average amount of dioxin in Agent Orange to be 13 ppm, while Jack Weinstein, for purposes of his ruling, decided that the average was 10 ppm. Dow and Hercules produced the 'cleanest' Agent Orange, while Monsanto and Diamond Alkalide made the 'dirtiest.'

"So, according to Weinstein, you have a substance that is 999, 990 parts harmless herbicide, and ten parts poison. He didn't like it when we characterized dioxin as a 'poison.' And he said that (I'm quoting him here) 'international conventions prohibit the use of chemical weapons, and if the chemical companies used dioxin, a poison, that would have been a violation of international law.'

"According to the companies, herbicides landed on the trees in Vietnam, and when it rained, the defoliants washed away. Unfortunately, we dumped over twenty million gallons over ten years.

"Scientists don't completely understand the causes of cancer—could be genetics, substance abuse, living near toxic waste dumps—but they have developed the ability to study an individual's genetic system, and some people seem to be genetically immune to dioxin, while others appear to be susceptible. So if you perform a study on exposure to dioxin in which you consider a person's genetic system, you may get a very good idea of an individual's susceptibility to toxic chemicals. Since no such studies have been performed in Vietnam, for now we have to rely on other forms of proof.

"Carcinogens and teratogens increase one's chances of giving birth to deformed children or developing cancer. If exposure to a toxin makes it twice as likely that you're going to develop an illness, then it's obvious that the drug increases the incidences of developing that illness, and it probably caused the illness.

"If you can prove that there's a doubling of birth defects or cancer after you've been exposed to a chemical, then for the purposes of our legal system, you've proven that there's a greater than fifty percent chance of correlation. It doubles your chance of getting an illness. And what's important here is that if you have 1,000 Vietnam veterans, you're not to going to see all of them come down with cancer. All of their children are not going to be born with birth defects. What you're going to find out is that maybe five of these veterans will die young from cancer, but what you are going to see is that out of those exposed to Agent Orange, maybe twelve or thirteen are going to die young from cancer.

"To a lay person, that might not be a big difference, but to a scientist that's a huge difference. If you can isolate that, and make sure that those twelve are not dying from something else, then that could be a statistically significant result. If you researched even this small sample, and you have twelve instead of five veterans dying young, then you may have proven your case."

The subway squeaks, rattles, and shakes its way through Manhattan, dips under the East River and rolls into the vast stretches of Brooklyn.

In 1000 BC, Chinese armies used arsenic smoke in battle; 600 BC, Assyrians poisoned enemy water supplies with rye ergot; 429–424 BC, Spartans used flames and toxic smoke created by burning wax and sulfur against Athens and its allies; 82–72 BC, Romans used "toxic smoke" against the Charakitanes in Spain, causing pulmonary problems and blindness; in 1763, the British gave smallpox-infected blankets to Indians at Fort Pitt, Pennsylvania; 1915–1916, the Germans used chlorine gas against Allied forces at Ypres; British forces retaliated with chlorine gas, to which the Germans responded with mustard gas; from 1937–1945, Japan used gas and bacteriological weapons in China; 1939–1945, Germans, Austrians, and Japanese poisoned, burned, starved, shot, and conducted experiments on human beings; 1987–1989, Iraq used chemical weapons against its Kurdish minority population.[7]

The Hague Convention IV and the 1925 Geneva Protocol were designed to prevent nation-states from using biological and chemical weapons against their adversaries in warfare. Unfortunately, those responsible for the manufacture of Agent Orange and the use of this herbicide in Vietnam treat these treaties like linguistic pawns in a game of high-stakes legal and financial chess. I wonder what the stockholders in highly profitable corporations like Dow and Monsanto feel about this game.

It appears that the chemical companies have outsmarted Vietnam veterans, the Vietnamese, hard-working, dedicated, brilliant lawyers, and powerful law firms. They played by the rules, and they won. But think again. Better yet, spend an afternoon watching lawyers who work for these companies knock about in the Realm. It won't take you long to discover that they appear to cast spells over the courtroom, forcing learned judges to follow the bouncing Orwellian ball. You might laugh, but not too loud or the marshals will toss you out. You might cry, but make sure you don't do anything to interfere with the magic show.

On the way home, you might stop for a drink with friends. You will try to tell them about the Realm. They will ask a lot of questions, and you will do your best to be clear and precise and honest. The Realm, you will say, is a very strange, exotic, confusing, contradictory place. Impossible to believe, even when you see it.

CHAPTER 10

Free Fire Zone

It will take a long time to clarify the exact consequences of Agent Orange.

—Douglas Peterson, US Ambassador to Vietnam

Blind soldier

Cu Chi district, a short drive from our hotel in downtown Ho Chi Minh City, was the scene of fierce fighting during the war.

It was here that men from the 25th Infantry stumbled upon a labyrinth of tunnels stretching all the way from the outskirts of Saigon to the Cambodian border. Two hundred miles of tunnels (soldiers dubbed them the "IRT," after one of New York City's subway lines) dug by men and women using small shovels and even spoons. Inside of these tunnels, the people General William Westmoreland called "human moles" constructed sleeping quarters, storage facilities, hospitals, and factories for building facsimiles of American weapons. Year after year, "tunnel rats" crawled into dark, fetid, dangerous holes, trying to find and kill these "moles." The military pumped CS gas into Cu Chi's tunnels, planted explosives inside of them, and tried to flood them, hoping to destroy the enemy's ability to pop out of the ground, to wound and kill unsuspecting Americans, and then to vanish without a trace.[1]

In the late 1950s, Ngo Dinh Diem, the anticommunist aristocrat the Eisenhower administration had installed as "President" of "South Vietnam," launched a reign of terror in Cu Chi district, arresting, torturing, jailing, and killing perceived opponents of his tyrannical regime, including thousands of Vietminh who'd fought against the French colonialists. In December 1958, Diem's jailers fed poisoned bread to several hundred prisoners at a camp in Phu Loi, just a few miles from Cu Chi. At the village of Phuoc Hiep, north of Cu Chi town, Diem's troops fired into crowds of peaceful marchers. Diem's brother, Ngo Dinh Nhu, rounded up suspected communists and guillotined them in the public squares of small villages.[2]

Returning from a visit to Vietnam in May 1961, Vice-President Lyndon Johnson called Diem the "Winston Churchill of the decade . . . in the vanguard of those leaders who stand for freedom." South Vietnam, said President John F. Kennedy, was a "proving ground for democracy."[3]

In 1961, Ngo Dinh Nhu supervised the opening of the first "strategic hamlet" camps (the Vietnamese called these places concentration camps) in Cu Chi district. The strategy was to separate Vietnamese civilians from communist insurgents. The South Vietnamese Army and later the US military destroyed entire communities, killing farm animals, ruining crops, and herding peasants into crowded camps that lacked food, water, and sanitation facilities. Peasants in Cu Chi district simply walked out of these "hamlets" and went back to whatever might be left of their homes.

On November 2, 1963, Ngo Din Diem and his brother were murdered in a coup supported by the American ambassador to South Vietnam, Henry Cabot Lodge, Jr. In August 1964, Congress passed the "Gulf of Tonkin Resolution," giving President Johnson powers to expand the war in Vietnam.

Forty years later, the mangrove forests and jungles that once covered the Cu Chi district are gone, leaving a landscape that resembles the fields of Iowa rather than the wilds of Southeast Asia. We pass small houses, with brown hump-neck cows standing by the front door, as though waiting to be invited inside for a glass of green tea. Rice fields, water buffalo, chickens, ducks, tiny stores and cafés tucked into flowering shrubbery, children playing beside the roads: little evidence that Cu Chi district was bombed, burned, gassed, defoliated, and bulldozed every single day for a decade.

The old soldier wears a long-sleeved shirt and shorts. His feet are bare and when he talks he appears to be listening carefully to his own words. Once, he says, this area of Cu Chi was covered with mangrove forests and jungles. Then, the spray planes appeared, moving slowly and quite low over the trees, back and forth until everything shriveled up and died.

I watch the man's face, trying to guess what he must be

thinking or feeling. Does the sound of my voice trigger visions of ambushes, firefights, and death? He pulls at his right sleeve, touches his chest, and explains that two bullets are lodged in his body, one in his right arm, and the other a few inches from his heart. After fighting for fifteen years in the forests and rice paddies, swamps and tunnels, he was blinded during a battle at Saigon's Ton Son Hut airport. His wife serves glasses of green tea and returns to the next room to attend to their son.

Le Van Can fought first in the Cu Chi region, but moved on to other places after the forests were defoliated. In 1969, he says, the United States sprayed Agent Orange everywhere. Day after day, the planes appeared, showering the land with dioxin. He and the men in his unit tried to use their raincoats to protect them from defoliants, but the chemicals ate holes in their coats. Le Van Can's unit moved from place to place, but it was impossible to escape the spraying; there wasn't anywhere to hide.

He recalls that his skin got red and that it was difficult to sleep, but no one died or—so far as he knew at the time—got seriously ill from the spraying. It was only after the war that soldiers began to develop health problems. One man he knew came from Quang Tri, and when he returned home he fathered six children. Five of these children died. Many men he'd served with got sick and died after the war. He does not really know what caused their deaths, but he does recall a soldier who fathered one child, a daughter, who was born with a "big head." She did not live very long.

Le Van Can doesn't know whether his wife was exposed to Agent Orange, but since the US destroyed the forests in Cu Chi, she most likely ate food and drank water contaminated with dioxin.

Like all of the former soldiers we meet, our host speaks softly, without the slightest hint of bravado or, most peculiar to our American sensibilities, the tremble of anger in his voice. Perhaps, if I persisted, he might say something about the battles in which he fought, or the final push on April 30, 1975, into Saigon, ending forty years of war against the French colonialists and American armies.

I am well aware that some people still blame Vietnam for the war. They are angry because Lyndon Baines Johnson refused to drop an atomic bomb on Hanoi. They hate anyone who fought against the war, and they call veterans who fraternize with former Vietcong North Vietnamese traitors. They say the Vietnamese are still holding American prisoners of war.

This kind of thinking has been an impediment to finding the missing link that will prove, once and for all, that Agent Orange/dioxin maims and kills human beings. I came to Vietnam to write about that missing link, not to reopen wounds or

Le Van Can's son

to engage in futile arguments about a war that tore the heart out of my generation. I do not know, nor do I care to know, what men like Le Van Can might have done in the war. He and his family are living with the legacies of chemical warfare. We are human beings; that is our common bond; that is the only thing that should matter now.

Is there really any difference between the thirty-one-year-old invalid lying on a bamboo bed in Cu Chi and a personal friend of mine who joined the Marines when he was seventeen years old, was leading reconnaissance missions in the Northern I Corps when he was nineteen, and is now dying, slowly and painfully, from Agent Orange-related illnesses? Do American Agent Orange children deserve more help, more love and kindness, than those who lie twisted, blind, and deaf upon pallets and floors and bamboo beds throughout Vietnam?

Before he left for the war, Le Van Can fathered one normal child. When he returned, his wife carried three of their children. One died before it was born, another lived for several days, and still another survived for three years. Their son has lived for thirty-one years.

This man and his wife have allowed us to visit their home, where we photograph their seriously deformed son, and ask questions that must cause them pain. They survive through help from the Red Cross and donations from others. People come and go, curious to know if the stories they've heard about chemical warfare can possibly be true. Shocked by what they see and hear, they return home determined to help victims of Agent Orange. Sometimes these people follow through on promises to write their representatives, to raise money, or to do what they can to persuade the chemical manufacturers of Agent Orange to use some of their profits to help Vietnamese families.

Le Van Can lights a cigarette and we shake hands across the

concrete table at which we've been sitting. I ask our interpreter to say that I am sorry that Mr. Can and his family are suffering from the effects of chemical warfare. She talks for a long time, the blind man nods once and does not say anything more.

Many years before this trip to Vietnam, I spent an evening with a Vietnam veteran who served with a psychological warfare (PSYOPS) unit.

"We used to play tapes from loudspeakers," my host told me, "basically saying that the VC were telling the people that herbicides were making them sick and that the spraying was responsible for their miscarriages and illnesses. And the tapes would say that the VC are lying, that they just don't like the sprays because it makes it hard for them to hide, and that the VC are actually poisoning people's water so the people will think it's the herbicides that are making them sick.

"I was young and gung-ho at the time; so I just believed the propaganda we were feeding the people. We heard the Vietnamese complain. They talked about depressions, diarrhea, colds, rashes, and spontaneous abortions. But it was a war zone, and we just figured there were a lot of diseases that we had never heard of.

"Thinking back, I recall being struck by the number of children with cleft palates. And I suffered from the same things over and over, screaming pains in my joints, pains in my gut, blood in my urine, my feet going numb. But the hardest thing to deal with was the sudden depressions that came on you. You just wanted to go out into a field and stick a pistol in your mouth and pull the trigger."[4]

Years before the United States launched its scorched earth campaign in Vietnam, scientists for Dow Chemical, one of the principal manufacturers of Agent Orange, were aware that dioxin is teratogenic and fetotoxic in rats and mice. In numerous studies over a period of decades, scientists have repeatedly shown that laboratory animals exposed to minute quantities of dioxin suffer catastrophic consequences.

In an exhaustive research paper, "Association between Agent Orange and Birth Defects: Systematic Review and Meta-Analysis," the authors write:

> Results of this meta-analysis combining data from twenty-two studies support the hypothesis that exposure to Agent Orange is associated with a statistically significant increase in the risk of birth defects, with a significant heterogeneity of effects across study populations. The result complements a previous finding that the risk of spina bifida, a specific birth defect, was elevated with Agent Orange exposure.[5]

The results of their study were:

> consistent with previous animal studies. Indeed, the detrimental effect of dioxin on congenital malformations has been documented in animal studies in which dioxin was shown to act as either a teratogen or mutagen.
>
> For example, maternal exposure to dioxin resulted in cleft palate and hydronephrosis in mice and hamsters, intestinal hemorrhage and renal abnormalities in rats, 61 extra ribs in rabbits, and spontaneous abortions in monkeys.
>
> There is evidence that mutagenic effects of dioxin can take place at the genetic level. Dioxin was found to cause chromosomal anomalies in the bone marrow cells of some specific strains of rats and mice, and

stimulate RNA synthesis in rat liver. Evidence from animal studies indicates that the observed association between Agent Orange/dioxin and birth defects in humans seems biologically plausible.... among populations exposed to Agent Orange, an elevated incidence of birth defects may have occurred.... Findings from this meta-analysis support the hypothesis that exposure to Agent Orange is associated with a statistically significant increase in risk of birth defects. The biological mechanism of this association and methodological limitations of Vietnamese studies warrant the consideration of conducting a large-scale and well-designed study in heavily sprayed regions of Vietnam to further elucidate the etiology of the Agent Orange and birth defects relationship. Future studies need to include biological measures of exposure. The long half-life of dioxin makes this possible even now.[6]

Our interpreter tells the family goodbye and I attempt to thank the woman of the house for the tea, but she has gone into the next room to care for her son.

Walking along a path back to the road, we stop to admire neat rows of bright green vines, perhaps cucumbers, soaking up the sun. It is noon, we are hungry, and have no idea where we might be going next, or how the men who accompany us manage to arrange these meetings with the people who do not have telephones or computers. Brendan stops to adjust his camera.

"Jesus, dad, he's my age, isn't he?" he asks.

"Yes, he's your age," I say. "Thirty-one years old."

"Thirty-one years old."

"And all that time, he's just been there."

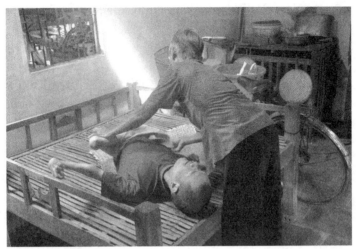

Mother and child

"Just there."

The ex-soldiers who accompany us climb into their car and we follow them along the dusty roads of Cu Chi district. Once, wild animals roamed this region's forests. We pass rice paddies, clumps of trees, heaps of rubbish. A dog. Two water buffalo. Overhead, the ubiquitous electric wires that mar Vietnam's natural beauty.

Testifying before a US Senate Committee on Veterans' Affairs, Maureen Ryan, whose husband served with the Marines in Vietnam, and whose daughter was born with at least sixteen birth defects, lamented the toll the war had taken on veterans' offspring.

"Just as truly as the bullets and bombs killed on the battlefields in Vietnam," said Mrs. Ryan, "maiming thousands of our men, Agent Orange has come home from those battlefields with our men. It has come home to maim and kill additional thousands of men who naively thought they had made it home safely. It would be tragic enough if it had ended there.

"But what the United States and what our Vietnam veterans did not know was that they carried home a tremendous legacy with them. They did not know that their children were with them on the battlefield, genetically. So Agent Orange is now reaping an additional harvest of birth defects and cancers in our children and men. We are losing our children through spontaneous abortions, through miscarriages, and perhaps most tragically in the surviving children, with the horrifying birth defects."[7]

Angered by the Veterans Administration's argument that it had not conducted an Agent Orange outreach program because it did not wish to confuse or frighten veterans and their wives, Ryan said, "It is not frightening when you are handed knowledge. It is much more frightening when you are kept in the dark. It is much more frightening to give birth to a child with birth defects. It is more frightening to know your husband is dying of cancer."[8]

In July 2009, the Bookworm bookstore in Hanoi invited me to give a public talk, at which I was asked what I thought about conducting more research studies on the effects of Agent Orange/dioxin on human beings. I answered that before we do any more studies we should find ways to help victims of the defoliation campaign. This upset one woman who argued that scientists need to crunch more numbers, juggle more statistics, and collect more evidence. But how long will it take to secure funding for these studies? And once this research is complete, exactly how many more years will it take for a panel to peer review the methodology and findings of a particular study?

Once a study is deemed credible, how long will it be before scientists working for the chemical companies attempt to discredit the researchers' findings? After five, ten, fifteen years, will the original study be tossed out or repeated, using altogether new methods for determining correlations between dioxin exposure and birth defects, cancer, and a host of other illnesses?

Meanwhile, the twisted body of a thirty-one-year-old man lies upon a bamboo pallet in Cu Chi district. His mother feeds him, changes his clothing, and massages his limbs to soothe the discomfort and pain he cannot describe. Are there one, two, five million victims of chemical welfare? Do the numbers matter? By the time more studies on the effects of Agent Orange/dioxin on human beings are completed, many more Vietnamese children will have died, leaving their parents to grieve and to wonder what their lives might have been like if their country had been allowed to live in peace.

CHAPTER 11

Chemical
Children

*These Agent Orange births are normal for us. . . . Every
now and then we have what we call a fetal catastrophe—
when the number of miscarriages and deformed babies, I
am afraid to say, overwhelms us.*

—Dr. Pham Viet Than, Tu Du Hospital

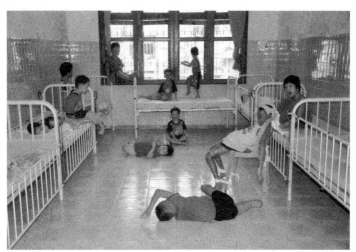

Agent Orange children in Tu Du Hospital.

To visitors, the quiet unassuming demeanor of Vietnamese people might be disconcerting. Given the costs of the war— between two and five million Vietnamese dead, several million victims of Agent Orange, including more than 150,000 children, hundreds of thousands of missing soldiers, broken promises, a prolonged and punishing trade embargo—one might expect anger, accusations, perhaps even insults. On the contrary, US veterans who return to the sites where they once fought vicious battles meet former enemies who welcome them as friends. The warriors get drunk together, sing, tell stories, and do what they can to heal the wounds of a long cruel war.

In the visitors' room at Tu Du, there's a display of books and pamphlets on Agent Orange, one with the peculiar title, "Cheer Up, Viet and Duc!" Inside of this book, there's a black and white photograph of Siamese twin boys connected at the waist, with one pair of legs and one set of genitals protruding from the point where the babies are attached. The twins, Viet and Duc, were born on February 25, 1981, in the Gialai-Kontum area in the Central Highlands, a heavily defoliated region of Vietnam. Terrified that they had given birth to "monsters," the boy's parents abandoned them, and the twins were flown to the Vietnam-East German Friendship Hospital, but they were quite ill and could not be separated. When they were twelve months old, they were taken to Tu Du Hospital in Ho Chi Minh City.

"The Tu Du Maternity Hospital," opens the book,

> stands in a beautiful place in Ho Chi Minh City, where red and white tropical flowers and blossoms bloom all the year round.
>
> Inside the hospital, about eight hundred women are

suffering, mostly from cancer, and every two days one deformed baby is born. This problem was probably caused by the herbicide containing dioxin, which the US used in the Vietnam War.

Since the US began to use this poison in 1961, more than twenty conjoined babies have been born in Vietnam, but most of them either were born dead or died within one year. Only Viet and Duc have barely survived. . . .

When I returned to my hotel and showed another Japanese a picture of Viet and Duc, he said very disgustedly, "Oh my goodness, why are such children kept alive?" I trembled with uncontrollable anger. Each and every human being has the right to live and develop.

The author decided to build a wheelchair for Viet and Duc, whom he describes as rather ordinary boys, in spite of the fact that they had the same organs in common, had to cooperate when urinating and excreting, and acknowledged that "it was certain that one's illness could be a great threat to the other's life."

Lying unstably, Viet and Duc made fun of each other. Viet was very playful and fond of fruit. Duc liked learning and had a sweet tooth. They both loved cars. Duc was physically weaker and usually lay down while Viet sat up. So Duc's side hair was worn out.[1]

When I attempt to return the book to the display case, Dr. Nguyen Thi Phuong Tan, director of rehabilitation of the Hoa Binh Village at Tu Du Hospital, politely insists that I must carry it home. But this book is a rare find, most likely out of print, the hospital's only copy. Dr. Tan smiles, her cell phone rings, I continue reading.

On October 4, 1988, a team of Japanese and Vietnamese doctors operated for fifteen hours at Tu Du Hospital to separate Viet and Duc. Viet survived twenty more years while Nguyen Duc still lives at the hospital.

Dr. Tan has been working in Tu Du hospital for twenty years, and she's been in charge of this "Peace Village" for twelve years. There are sixty children here, many with disabilities like missing fingers and toes, mental disabilities, and some with dysfunctions of the spinal cord. Dr. Tan explains that other children suffer from some dysfunction or unusual alteration in their DNA. Most of the children come from Quang Tri Province, the Central Highlands, Kontum, and other defoliated regions.

Dr. Tan thinks that some of the boys and girls in Peace Villages like Hoa Binh are third generation Agent Orange children. Some of them need operations to repair their deformed faces so they can work outside of the village. Those who are capable of learning attend classes in the hospital. If the children's parents fought in heavily sprayed areas, or if they were farmers there during the war, it's reasonable to assume, says Dr. Tan, that they were exposed to dioxin.

Critics dismiss this approach to determining the cause of birth defects found in Vietnamese children as "anecdotal." In one sense, as attorney Dean Kokkoris pointed out, they have a valid argument. Vietnamese researchers are not willing to feed human beings dioxin-laced rice. They have not injected dioxin into the bodies of perfectly healthy men and women. Scientists in other parts of the world refuse to treat human beings like lab rats. Until researchers give up their aversion to testing dioxin on human beings, the lawyers who work for the chem-

Showing off for visitors.

ical companies and the judges who preside over Agent Orange lawsuits will refuse to accept the argument that dioxin harms human beings.

During our travels, we have seen children with missing fingers, toes, arms, and legs; children with lobster claw hands, twisted feet, large heads, stunted bodies, strange dark blotches on their faces and arms, purple bark-like skin. We've heard parents talk about children whose brains seem to develop normally for a few years and then, for some inexplicable reason, this growth stalls, freezing the child's development at an early age, so that while he might resemble a quite ordinary Vietnamese adolescent, he can not perform simple tasks.

Like all of the Vietnamese doctors, scientists, and community workers with whom we meet, Dr. Tan is fully aware that some people refuse to believe that dioxin is responsible for the blind girl who spends her days banging her face against the slats of her crib; the boy whose watermelon head looks like it might explode; the teenage girl with missing arms who has learned to draw and write by holding a pencil between her toes; the small boy whose body stopped developing just below the waist, so he sits, half of him, huge brown eyes sad beyond sad; the little girl who scoots about the ward on chubby stumps that will never develop into legs.

"People come from all over the world to visit Tu Du's Peace Village," says Dr. Tan, "We ask them if they've ever seen any cases like the children in Vietnam that we are working with. And some of them say they have never seen a case like this. Others say yes, they have, but it is quite rare. These are doctors from around the world, Australia, Canada, France, and they see these children, and they know that they come from areas that were heavily sprayed with Agent Orange.

"I hope that when your book is published, the international community will then know what I, as a doctor, have seen all

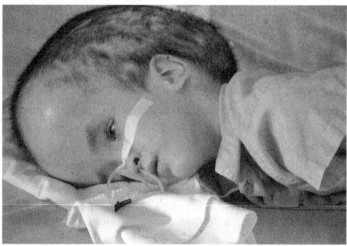

Boy with a large head.

these years—that Agent Orange was used in Vietnam, causing problems for people here, not just for the first generation, but for other generations."

"When Agent Orange was sprayed here," Dr. Tan continues, "it left a burden until now, so we have so many children suffering from Agent Orange, and it is a burden for the economy and for society. And I want to say that the ones who sprayed the Agent Orange have to be responsible for what they did in Vietnam. They have to compensate, and they have to help us to solve this problem. This is their responsibility."

In 1995, friends of Vietnam from the German city of Ober-

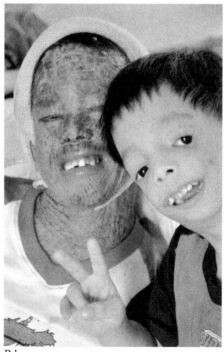

Pals

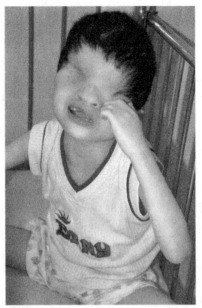

Girl born without eyes.

hausen established Peace Village at Tu Du Hospital, a place where Agent Orange children can live in a genuinely loving, supportive community. There are other peace villages in Ho Chi Minh City, Cu Chi, Danang, and Hanoi. In these villages, the staff gives the children love and treats them with kindness and dignity. Vietnam's Agent Orange children suffer from a variety of physical handicaps and mental disabilities, but this does not keep them from greeting us with laughter and hugs. They pose for pictures, want to be picked up, and show off like ordinary children, except they must scramble about on missing, deformed, and stunted limbs.

Duc enters the room in a wheelchair, and we talk briefly about the operation that separated him from Viet. He works as a computer technician at Peace Village and has been married for two years. Does he feel any anger toward the United States government or the chemical companies?

"No," he says. "I don't care about this. Because I know that if I get angry, nothing can change my life. I was born with such a situation, so what I'm doing now is to strive for my life. To try my best to have a good life."

Like Dr. Tan, he wants the chemical companies to do something to help people. Most people live in rural areas, and they have a difficult life, he says. So there must be some kind of action taken to help them.

Duc and his wife plan to have their first child this year. He leaves before we get a chance to ask him what they plan to name their new baby.

Dr. Tan motions for us to follow her and we do so without hesitation, having learned that the Vietnamese never bother to explain where we might be going. Over the course of our trip, we've taken taxis to buildings where we've been told to appear at a given time of day. A man gets into the taxi, and we drive through the streets of Danang stopping to pick up other people, most often young women who are not unfriendly, but who never introduce themselves or explain why they are joining us. After a while, you get used to being driven here and there, getting out, getting back in. At first, following Dr. Tan through this hospital feels no different. But at the end of the hall, she opens the door to a room where the monsters are kept.

Boy missing hands and feet.

CHAPTER 12

Evidence Room

As a young intern in Saigon's Tu Du Hospital, Dr. Nguyen Thi Ngoc Phuong loved delivering babies to mothers. The year was 1963, and President Ngo Dinh Diem was mounting a reign of terror in the city and countryside. Buddhist monks were marching through the streets to protest Diem's brutal attacks on them. In one such action, Thich Quang Duc sat down at a Saigon intersection and clasped his hands in prayer as a fellow monk doused him with gasoline, and another monk touched a lighter to his saffron robe. Duc sat upright, unmoving until his lifeless body collapsed into the street. A photograph of this burning monk appeared on the front page of newspapers throughout the world.

Asked how she felt about these protests, Madame Nhu, the "dragon lady" wife of Diem's brother, called the self-immolations "barbecues," and vowed to clap whenever monks died that way.

Dr. Phuong continued working in the hospital's maternity ward, bringing red-faced, wrinkled, crying babies into the world. To Dr. Phuong, this was the natural cycle of life: Mothers give birth to babies; babies grow up, get married, and have families of their own; people grow old and die.

"I didn't know anything about the spraying," says Dr. Phuong, "And nothing about Agent Orange. But one day—it was 1969—I delivered for the first time in my life a severely deformed baby. It had no head or arms. The mother didn't see her child, and I tried to hide my tears and my fear from her. I couldn't bring myself to tell her what the baby looked like, so I said it was very weak. It died, and I just told her that it had been too weak to live."

Dr. Phuong delivered more and more babies with missing limbs, two bodies fused together with one set of internal organs; babies with partial or missing brains, missing heads, babies that didn't open their eyes, didn't cry, and died within a few days after delivery. Instead of fully formed fetuses, some women at Tu Du gave birth to formless bloody lumps. In late 1967, following a period of massive use of Agent Orange in Vietnam,

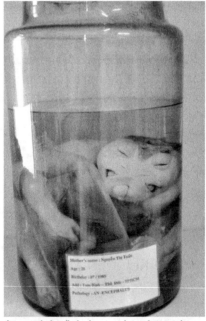

Anencephalus (baby born with a substantial part of its brain missing).

Saigon newspapers began publishing reports on a new birth abnormality, calling it the "egg bundle-like fetus." Photographs of this "egg bundle" appeared on the front page of some South Vietnam newspapers. One paper, *Dong Nai* published an article about women giving birth to stillborn fetuses, with a photograph of a dead baby whose face was that of a duck. A day later, *Dong Nai* ran a story about a woman giving birth to a baby with "two heads, three arms, and twenty fingers." Just above the article, the paper posted a photograph of another deformed baby with a head that resembled that of a poodle or a sheep. Still another Saigon newspaper, *Tia Sang*, on June 26, 1969, printed a picture of a baby with "three legs, a head squeezed in close to the legs, and two arms wrapped around a big bag that replaced the lower section of the face . . ."[1]

The Saigon government's counterargument was that these birth defects were caused by something it called "Okinawa bacteria."[2]

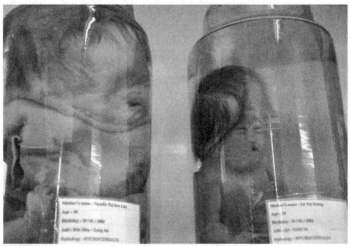

Hydrocephalus (babies born with water on the brain).

I've read about Dr. Phuong's work for many years, and consider it an honor that she has taken the time to talk about what must be, even after all these years, a painful subject. For some people, this would be an opportunity to launch into a monologue about being misunderstood, marginalized, and ridiculed. But the Vietnamese with whom we meet rarely talk about themselves, and they never complain. When they do speak of their efforts to convince skeptics that the Vietnamese have suffered catastrophic injuries as a result of chemical warfare, it is without the slightest hint of self-aggrandizement or self-pity.

Dr. Phuong wanted people to know about the increasing number of deformed babies she and other staff were seeing in Tu Du Hospital's delivery room.

"So I contacted a newspaper," she smiles. "One that was not part of the regime at the time, but people didn't really believe me. Not in the South, anyway. Only in Hanoi did I have any real support. People there were far less skeptical about what the spraying was doing to people in Vietnam."

Dr. Phuong could not have known that soon after the United States military commenced full-scale use of Agent Orange in Vietnam, Dow Chemical, one of the principal manufacturers of this herbicide, invited representatives from other companies to attend an urgent meeting. Once there, Dow revealed that Agent Orange contained TCDD-dioxin, the most toxic chemical company researchers had ever encountered.

Dow's scientists believed that TCDD-dioxin was one hundred times as toxic as Parathion, a chemical that Rachel Carson described in *Silent Spring* as an organic phosphate, "one of the most powerful and dangerous."[3]

Dow called a meeting and advised those present—Hooker Chemical, Hercules, and Diamond Alkali—not to reveal what they might know about the harmful effects of dioxin. If the government found out about the potential dangers of this chemical, it might impose regulations on the production of herbicides.

While Dr. Phuong struggled with how to console young mothers who'd given birth to hopelessly deformed babies, scientists in the US discovered that even in the lowest doses given, 2,4,5-T, one of the herbicides in Agent Orange, caused cleft palates, missing and deformed eyes, cystic kidneys, and enlarged livers in the offspring of laboratory animals. The results of this study would be withheld until 1969, the year Dr. Phuong spared a young mother from knowing that she had given birth to a monster.

In 1971, Thomas Whiteside published *The Withering Rain,* an early look at the use of herbicides in Vietnam. A careful, scrupulous researcher, Whiteside set out to speak with officials at Dow Chemical and government scientists he assumed would be forthcoming about the effects of herbicides on human beings and the environment.

"I was hardly surprised," writes Whiteside,

> to find officials of the Dow Chemical Company, one of the largest manufacturers of 2,4,5-T, uncommunicative. But I was taken aback to encounter plain antagonism from several scientists connected with the government when I raised with them what I thought were reasonable questions about the way in which information on the studies of the teratogenic, or fetus deforming, activity of 2,4,5-T in experimental animals had been handled. They intimated that such matters were beyond the understanding of laymen and comprehensible only to professional biologists.

"I found this kind of attitude disappointing," continued Whiteside in characteristic understatement,

> in people who I had supposed were devoted to the search for scientific truth. I formed the suspicion that this professional grandiosity was in part something very like a cover for timidity—a reluctance to discuss even a prima facie case against potentially dangerous compounds for fear of a whipping by professional critics at the next scientific convention.

Dismayed by the cavalier attitude of an official at the laboratory where scientists discovered that "2,4,5-T exerted clearly teratogenic effects on experimental mice and rats," Whiteside notes, "what we were talking about was a spray rate of 2,4,5-T that, at least as laid down in Vietnam, could result in a pregnant Vietnamese woman's ingesting close to an equivalent amount of 2,4,5-T that, in experimental rats, deformed one out of three of the rats' unborn offspring."[4]

Dr. Phuong sketches a picture of a "mole baby," a large egg shape, open at one end, containing "bloody liquid." Inside of the egg shape she draws many small circles, labeling them "frogs legs." Beside her drawing, she writes: *hydatidiform mole, chorio carcinoma.*

"I was very much criticized by my colleagues," says Dr. Phuong. "I saw the babies, and I knew that sooner or later people would begin to believe me, but it took ten years until they did. I just felt the need to find out what was wrong, and I wanted to do something to help the parents and the children.

"It was really only after 1975 that we began to know more about the consequences of Agent Orange. It was hard at that time to find a lot of documentation about the effects of herbicides on the environment and people. Bert Pfeiffer and Arthur Westing from the National Academy of Science had conducted research in Vietnam and Cambodia, but most of their work centered on the effects of herbicides on plant life, rather than human beings. In March 2006, at the International Conference of Victims of Agent Orange held in Hanoi, Vietnam, former Marine Daniel J. Shea talked about his son, Casey, who was born with congenital heart disease, a cleft palate, and stomach abnormalities. When Casey was three years old, doctors told the family that he needed a shunt in his heart to help the flow of oxygen, but the child went into a coma during surgery and later died in his father's arms.

"What right," a tearful Daniel Shea asked the audience, "does anyone have to make chemical potions to poison the land and its people? . . . Is it not criminal, even in times of war, to poison a people's food crops? The world has condemned chemical warfare because it takes not only enemy soldiers, but innocent men, women, and children alike . . . and it cripples generation after generation of those exposed to its toxins."[5]

"Our mission was a sad one," wrote Dr. Westing, after touring defoliated parts of Cambodia,

> A mission whose *raison d'être* we wish had never occurred. We felt particularly grieved about the innumerable direct and indirect losses suffered by the innocent local populace. We were able to see at first hand how particularly pernicious this type of military action is for people whose very existence is so closely tied to the land. And now that since the time of our visit the whole area we came to know has been utterly destroyed by the full impact of the spreading air and ground war, our sadness has turned to a feeling of despair.[6]

Long before Daniel Shea's moving testimony, Dr. Phuong delivered for the first time in her life a baby that had no head or limbs. After that, she witnessed terrible birth defects every few days. She watched new mothers go into shock when they saw their babies. She listened to them cry, sometimes for days, and heard them lament that they must have committed some terrible mistake for which God was punishing them.

"It took ten years for people to believe me," says Dr. Phuong.

After the war ended in 1975, veterans began visiting the hospital to ask about birth defects and cancers related to herbicide spraying. She learned a lot from them, and they formed a bond that helped her continue working on behalf of Agent Orange children.

"What happened in Vietnam," says Dr. Phuong, "was the first time in human history that a country has used chemical weapons, for so many years, on such a massive scale. This must never be allowed to happen again. Ever. We conducted many studies at Tu Du Hospital on the effects of Agent Orange, and scientists in other countries have conducted studies as well. We know that Dr. Arnold Schecter found high levels of dioxin in Vietnamese mothers' milk, and that dioxin, like other toxic chemicals, can move from the mother's body, through the placenta, into the developing fetus. We know that there are 'hot spots' in Vietnam, where high levels of dioxin have been found, and where dioxin has gotten into the food chain, so that people have been eating ducks and fish contaminated with dioxin."

Does she invite manufacturers of Agent Orange to visit Tu Du Hospital, and to examine the extensive research she and other Vietnamese doctors and scientists have done into the effects of dioxin on animals and human beings?

"Oh yes," she smiles, "I've invited them many times to visit.

But they don't come. They don't talk. They hide. I always think that they do believe me. And that some day the United States government and the chemical companies will agree to help victims of Agent Orange. But if the companies refuse to pay, then people should not buy their products. All over the world, people should boycott those companies."

It is late afternoon, and our interpreter looks tired. For the past three days, Miss Minh has accompanied us to homes in Cu Chi district, to Peace Village 2 in Ho Chi Minh City, and now to the Ngoc Tam Hospital where Dr. Phuong is general director. Witnessing the legacies of chemical warfare—handicapped children, poverty-stricken families, and jars containing horribly deformed fetuses—can be exhausting, indeed overwhelming, not only because of what we've seen, but because of the emotional roller coaster on which we've been riding, descending into a deep sadness, roiling in despair, rising to a rage that collapses into sullen confusion and a feeling of helplessness.

If you happen to visit Friendship Village in Hanoi, and the Peace Villages in Danang and Ho Chi Minh City, you will probably want to call your elected representatives, your prime minister or president, the heads of chemical companies to demand that they drop whatever they may be doing and come, quickly, to Vietnam. You will want to take one, or all, of these children home.

Dr. Phuong has testified at many international conferences on dioxin, she has published numerous scientific papers, and spoken to members of Congress about the need to help victims of chemical warfare. She does not believe that more studies are necessary to prove that dioxin harms human beings.

We descend the stairs to a small entranceway. Dr. Phuong

is delighted to find her granddaughter waiting, and as they prepare to ride a motorbike into the chaotic Ho Chi Minh traffic, she calls out:

"I'm sixty years old. And still delivering babies."

If the monsters in the Evidence Room could speak, what might they say? Would they want to know who poisoned their mothers and fathers? Did their mothers manage to give birth to normal babies, or, like so many Vietnamese women, did their children stop eating, grow listless, and—like Dr. McNulty's rhesus monkeys—just lie down and die? Are their fathers still alive? Men who came home from the war in seemingly good health, wishing only to put the war behind them, and then one day started to feel weak, chronically exhausted, hammers driving nails into their brains, mole-like growths erupting over their limbs, chests, and backs. Sometimes their bodies itch, not just their skin, but like swarms of insects gnawing at their insides. Unable to work, these men become invalids, confined to bed. Doctors tell ex-soldiers that their bodies are diseased; they have weak hearts, cancer, and other ailments for which there is no cure. They will die from having been exposed for many years to Agent Orange.

Dr. Phuong has met many doubters. She's listened to their arguments, and she understands that the adage, "seeing is believing," does not always hold true. She also knows that reputable scientists in many countries now share her views about the deadly effects of dioxin. The chemical companies may try to discredit Dr. Phuong's work, and that of other researchers like her, but she does not intend to give up her decades-long struggle to convince doubters that Agent Orange/dioxin has mutilated and killed many thousands of babies inside of their mothers' wombs.

CHAPTER 13

Letters Don't Lie

War reverberates for years afterward, spinning lives into a
dark oblivion of pain and suffering.

—Chris Hedges

Ken Herrman landed on Hill 435, better known as LZ West, during the battle for Nui Cham Mountain. Grunts were pulling body bags off choppers, helping the walking wounded, and tossing supplies onto departing birds. It was May 1968, four months after the Vietcong and the North Vietnamese army had attacked every town and city in the southern half of Vietnam, sustaining heavy losses but still capable of waging fierce attacks against American forces.

Herrmann was assigned to operate a radio at night, communicating with infantry companies in the valley below LZ West.

"The operations officer for the battalion was an insomniac who spent hours each night discussing the war, philosophy, literature, and the madness in which we were all immersed. One night he asked me what I'd like to do during the war. I said, 'leave and go home.' He laughed and asked if I'd like to work with the Vietnamese in the valley. I'd been a teacher and a social worker before being drafted, and he thought this was a good background for doing that."

Herrmann soon found himself trudging along with infantrymen throughout the valley and west from the Que Son Valley into Hiep Duc Valley, an area heavily controlled by the Vietcong.

As Civil Affairs officer for the battalion, he organized medcaps (medical clinics for the locals), distributed propaganda posters, and broadcasted propaganda over backpack loudspeakers to lure the enemy into surrendering.

"I was briefly assigned the responsibility for psychological operations. That meant that I became the disc jockey for the valley. I carried a thirty-pound speaker system on my back and a cassette recorder in my pack. Accompanied by an interpreter, I would crawl around in the night, broadcasting the names of suspected Vietcong and playing loud Vietnamese love songs to make the VC so homesick they would stop fighting. During a few firefights, we played these songs and read the names. The music did not seem to have any effect on the fighters at all. It did have an effect that we could measure just once. We sat on a hill, played tunes, and begged the enemy to surrender for a straight twenty-four hours. The next day, US troops were shocked to see thirty VC holding their weapons in the air and surrendering. I never knew if they could not stand the music we chose, and surrendering seemed the only way to stop us from playing it, or we actually broke their morale."

Herrmann became the liaison between Saigon regime troops and his unit. Then, accompanied by about fifty South Vietnamese soldiers, he relocated to a small knoll along the Tu Bon River. His mission was to establish a displaced persons' village farther west than his unit had ever gone.

During the following months, Herrmann resettled thousands of people and arranged for food distribution, medical care, housing construction, a school, and assistance from agricultural experts.

"This was my village," he recalls. "These were my people. The battalion created a no-fire zone around Hiep Duc Village. Troops firing at my people were seen by me as the enemy. They were attacking what quickly became my family. An odd family it was. The people were malnourished. Most had malaria and severe skin disorders. A number had leprosy. Many bore the scars of battle. A four-year-old girl wandered in one morning with her brain exposed; somehow still able to walk. An American grenade had blown off part of her skull.

"I wasn't a very skilled warrior. The first time under fire I was with a rifle platoon near the village. There was the sound of something flying quickly by my ear. People were screaming, 'sniper,' and I just lay on the ground while grunts fired on full automatic into the trees and bushes. Silence, and a soldier joking, 'Man, you almost bought it.' That round missed me by less than an inch. I can still hear the sound."

Herrmann still finds it hard to believe that the military would give him, a reluctant warrior, the responsibility for about 2,000 people who were malnourished, frightened, wounded, and ridden with malaria and other diseases.

"This was Hiep Duc in 1968–1969. Almost daily mortar attacks, snipers, firefights. Imagine having absolutely no idea what to do in such a position, just flying by the seat of your pants. The military never acknowledged my ignorance. The US Army informed me that I knew what to do, and that I was doing a good job. I agreed. Completely."

The military thought it always knew more than the Vietnamese, and this self-righteous attitude made Herrmann and other soldiers feel successful. He was awarded a Bronze Star and the Saigon government's Cross of Gallantry. One month after he arrived home, the valley exploded in some of the fiercest fighting of the war. Herrmann wondered who had received his .45 pistol and M-16, and if that soldier, and the one after that, had survived the war.

"I was met by relatives at the Buffalo airport. My nephew was about nine and asked me at the airport what I had done in the war. His father said, 'We won't talk about this.' I didn't until years later. I drank for medicinal purposes, relived fire-fights and insanity each night, and pretended the war I carried with me had ended with my return in 1969. It did not."

In 1998, a couple of friends asked Herrmann if he would travel to Vietnam with them. At first, he refused, but in time he agreed to go.

"We spent much of our time," laughs Herrmann, "hiding in hotels, and the rest visiting places where we had served. I returned to Hiep Duc."

At first, he didn't recognize the village where he'd lived for a year. Foliage hid the ravages of war; he couldn't smell defoliants or napalm. People told him that the tin smells in the air and the off-green color of the countryside were due to dioxin.

"I knew this was my old village when I saw the familiar riverbanks, the small knoll where I'd lived in a culvert, a sandbagged hole; and the surrounding mountains on which so much American and Vietnamese blood had been shed. This was the place that local myth taught was filled with the unsettled spirits of the thousands who had died liberating their nation."

This was the beginning of Ken Herrmann's healing. He wanted to learn about Vietnamese history, culture, religious practices, and literature. He hoped to get to know the people his generation had been taught to hate and trained to kill. He hoped one day to create a study abroad program for students at SUNY Brockport, the college where he was a Social Work professor. A few years later, he managed to do just that.

In this program, students spend a semester in Danang studying Vietnamese language, culture and history, offering English language lessons to Vietnamese children, visiting and assisting Agent Orange families, and delivering food and other supplies to a leper colony accessible by boat.

Herrmann wants students to get out of the classroom and meet Vietnamese people, to experience Vietnam's 4,000 year-old culture, and to understand the toll that decades of warfare have taken on Vietnam. At one point, he wrote an article in a Vietnamese newspaper suggesting that people write to him about the effects of Agent Orange on their families. Letters poured in from all over the country, and before long he had boxes filled with more than 4,000 accounts of suffering and urgent pleas for help from men, women, and children.

In some cases, the letter-writer was exposed to Agent Orange while fighting in the war. In others, writers were the children or grandchildren of parents who ate food and drank water contaminated with Agent Orange.

Herrmann calls these letters "a chronicle of courage, determination, and hope. They are also an account of illness, poverty, bewilderment, and despair. Writers want to know why the country that waged a scorched earth campaign in Vietnam is unwilling to help them. Has America forgotten about Vietnam? Is Agent Orange/dioxin mutagenic? How many years, how many victims, will it take for Vietnam to be free of the curse of dioxin?"

LETTERS

Nam Dinh, June 02, 2004
To: SUNY Brockport from a rural village in North Vietnam.

Before April 1975, my husband fought in the Liberation Army in South Eastern Vietnam. Agent Orange affected him during this time. We married after he came back from the war. We have three children who are also affected by Agent Orange. All three of them are paralyzed. They cannot do anything by themselves. I have to be around to provide twenty-four-hour care.

Although we are receiving care and assistance from the local government, this still is not enough to recover from this endless pain.

I suggest that your program send these letters to the US president, the Americans, and the company producing this deadly agent. They must be aware of our ongoing pain and should officially apologize to my people and compensate for what they have caused in my country."

Thank you,

Bui Thi Bon

■ ■ ■

To Prof. Kenneth Herrmann, director
SUNY Brockport Veteran Program

I am writing this letter in response to the appeal you made in the Thanh Nien Newspaper on May 24, 2004.

My name is Ho Van Xanh. I was born in 1936 in Phuoc Son Hiep Duc, Quang Nam. I am from the ethnic minority group.

During the war between the US and Vietnam, I saw the US helicopters dumping Agent Orange onto my hometown. Right after that all of the plants and vegetables were killed. I am an ethnic minority group so I spent all of my life in the mountainous area. I ate vegetables and drank water from this area. I have had arthritis since 1975. It is getting worse over time. My granddaughter was born in 2002. When she was born she had little black moles on her skin. Over time, these black spots have gotten much bigger. They cover the right side of her body, are on her face, legs and arms, and are still spreading. On these black areas she is also growing fur similar to an animal. Thank you.

Ho Van Xanh

■ ■ ■

Professor Kenneth Herrmann
Director of the SUNY Brockport Vietnam Program

I am Le Quang Chon. I am 54 years old.
I would like to present my family's circumstances.
I joined the Vietnamese People's Army and fought at the Tay Nguyen Battlefield for national independence.
I have been infected with Agent Orange used by the US Army in Vietnam. In consequence of this my wife has had three monsters in three pregnancies followed by three disabled children:
—Le Thi Thoa: Congenitally amputated.
—Le Quang Chien: disabled and deformed
—Le Quang Chuong: disabled left leg (Cannot move.)
The photos of our three children are attached to this letter.

For me, I have been infected directly with Agent Orange: poor eyesight, losing most of my lower jaw's teeth, two loose teeth, often getting ill, gastrectomy of three-fourths of my stomach, gangrene of forty cm of my intestine, rheumatic limbs, neurasthenia.

My wife is in panic when seeing such a husband and children. Therefore, she has a mental disease. Sometimes, she does not know what she is doing. My family has too many difficulties in both material and spiritual life. My family members have suffered from the effects of the Agent Orange. Therefore, we have to speak up in order that the world people know the Agent Orange victims' losses.

Yours,

Le Quang Chon
Trinh Nga Hamlet

■ ■ ■

Hoang Trinh Commune,
Hoang Hoa District, Thanh Hoa Province

Dear Professor Kenneth Herrmann,

My name is Tran Thi Lanh. I was born and raised in Trieu Phong, Quang Tri. This area was mercilessly destroyed by chemical warfare during the American war.

My daughter is two years old but she cannot speak or sit up. Her head is getting bigger while her muscles are getting smaller. Our life is very difficult. We have to live off of my parents and my neighbors.

I know that you are collecting letters from across Vietnam. I hope that my daughter will be another proof to illustrate the disastrous effects of the AO the American soldiers used during the war.

Thank you.

Tran Thi Lanh

▪▪▪

Dear Professor Herrmann,

My name is Phan Phuoc Trung and I am fifty-five years old.

My wife's name is To Thi Dieu and she is fifty years old.

I was very touched to read the appeal that you made in the newspaper. The article came to me like an angel's arrival to save the lives of millions of AO victims in my country.

We, the AO victims in Vietnam, really appreciate your concern for us. The war has been over for almost thirty years. The Americans have begun to forget about us while millions of the Vietnamese people are still living with its disastrous effects. It is a tragedy. There are millions of Vietnamese families who are living with persistent pain caused by the American troops during the war. There are many families, Dear Mr., that are affected into the third generation. We still have no idea when AO will stop affecting the health and safety of my innocent people. It may affect the fourth and fifth generations. The list may be longer.

Dioxin still exists in the soil we cultivate, the water we drink, and the food we eat. This means that it sill exists within each Vietnamese citizen.

The US government has admitted the effect of AO on the American troops who served in the Vietnam War. The veterans have been compensated. It is unjust with the AO victims.

All of the Vietnamese AO victims have been living in silence. They are lonely, coping with their pains and losses. The company producing this deadly agent must be responsible for this. It is time for us to share with you our pains.

Yes, I am going to share with you the story of my family. My wife and I were born and raised in Hue. We married and had five healthy and good-looking children before we moved to Ninh Son, Ninh Thuan Province in 1994. By the end of 1995, our daughter named Phan Thi My Lien was born. We were miserable to know that Lien had a cleft lip and that her head was flat. She is nine years old now, but she cannot walk, cannot speak, and cannot recognize anything. She weighs ten kilos (22 pounds). We were very nervous and were told that the place where we were living was heavily sprayed with AO during the American War. We immediately sold our house and moved to a different place. A couple of years ago, I came back to this place to visit my neighbors. I discovered that the family who had bought my house also gave birth to a disabled child. Their son is mentally retarded. I also learned that the midwife who helped with Lien's arrival also had two disabled children. Both of them had died. In addition to this, there are many disabled children in this area.

I just shared with you the story about my family. This is just one of millions of stories about AO victims in Vietnam. Please communicate to any people you know about how deadly this agent is.

Many thanks.

Phan Phuoc Trung

Truc Ninh, Nam Dinh, May 31, 2004

■ ■ ■

Dear Professor Kenneth Herrmann,

I would like to tell you the story about my family. My father came from a poor family. He joined the Liberation Army in November 1969 and became a tank driver. He traveled across Southern Vietnam. He came back home in September 1975, rejoined the army in September 1987, and came back home shortly after that. He then married my mother. A year after my parents were married, my sister, Nguyen Thi Xuan, was born. When she was five days old, she began to have seizures. My parents sent her to many hospitals in the area but it did not help. She was paralyzed. My mother had to stop working to provide care to my sister.

Two years later I was born. The same symptoms occurred: half of my body was paralyzed. Life became more difficult.

When my father was forty-six years old, he was diagnosed with cancer and passed away shortly after that. All the family's belongings were sold for his medication and treatment.

My mother became a single mother with two disabled children when she was thirty-eight years old. It has been twenty-three years. My mother has heart disease but she has to work very hard for us.

I am luckier than my sister is. I am a tailor. Nevertheless, I still find it hard to integrate into the community. People seem to ignore me and make fun of my disability.

I have attached a picture of my sister. I wish you good health.

Thanks.

Nguyen Thi Vien

■ ■ ■

Dear Professor Kenneth Herrmann,

The war has been over for almost thirty years. However, the disastrous effects are still there in every corner of Vietnam. It is heartbreaking to think about the large amounts of dioxin that was sprayed by American troops from 1964 to 1975.

I was born during the time American troops were spraying dioxin. My name is Nguyen Thi Hong and I was born in 1955. I currently live in Trung Nam hamlet, Que Trung commune, Que Son district, Quang Nam Province.

I was a common resident who was living in the area where American troops sprayed dioxin. At that time the weather became increasingly hot and famine was widespread. However, both the food and water were badly contaminated. Regardless of the spraying, we drank the water without paying any attention to its pungent smell. We also ignored side effects such as headaches and dizziness. I didn't think about the long-term effects.

I gave birth to my only child in 1995. Her name is Nguyen Thi Thuy Van. Unfortunately, she suffered from malnourishment. She did not recognize any movements until she was two years old. In addition to her mental state, she also has an inborn heart defect; this serious disease is always life-threatening.

Since this time our economic condition has dramatically gotten worse. I have been spiritually devastated knowing that my only child is in danger. As a widow, I don't know what to do to help my daughter. It is most miserable to know that the poisonous water I drank when I was young is the cause of her disease. The poison has passed from my genes to hers.

I am very glad to read about your appeals. I write this letter with the hope that you will help us. Ask the American government and dioxin manufacturers to be responsible for these disastrous effects.

My family as well as millions of Vietnamese Agent victims is very grateful for your concern and kindness. I wish you great health.

Nguyen Thi Hong
Trung Nam
Que Trung, Queue Son, Quant Nam,
Vietnam, July 21st 2004

■ ■ ■

Dear Prof. Kenneth Herrmann,
　With reference to your article titled "Vietnamese AO victims need to say" in Labour newspaper, I write this letter to share our situation with you and your program.
　In the war from 1964 to 1975, my husband was a driver in the army. He was stationed at A Sau. A Luoi.
　We had had two normal children (one son, one daughter) before he joined in the South battlefield. However, after coming back from the war we had one more child in 1980. Unfortunately, she was abnormal. She's only 13 kilos weight, keeps crying days and nights. I went to have her cured, but it was useless because the doctors all said that she was born mentally retarded. She was blind, paralyzed. She realized nothing about the world around her. I was so sad to know that dioxin from her father's body had passed to hers causing her diseases.
　Now she is twenty-five years old, but she is only a child. She knows nothing except crying. I have to help her with everything in her daily activities. My family, therefore, meets with too many difficulties.
　As far as I am concerned, you and the "SUNY Brockport Vietnam" program want to aid AO victims. I write this letter

with the hope that you will help us to partly compensate for the great losses that were caused by American troops in the war.

Finally, I wish you and your colleagues health and success. Many thanks!

Nguyen Thi Cam Bao
102 D4 Vong Cau Giay, Ha Noi

■ ■ ■

Dear Prof. Kenneth Herrmann

My family are AO victims.

My Professor, I am Nguyen Quynh Loc, born in 19(?). I joined army at the battlefield of the South in 1972. At 1977 I went North. After I had completed my mission, I came back and got married.

We have three children. The eldest daughter is Nguyen Thi Huong Giang, born in 1988. She has a nervous disease.

The second is a boy. Nguyen Minh Phu, born 1990. He has no arm.

The last son is Nguyen Duc Tho, born in 1993. He has myasthenia, gets worse nutrition, has difficulty growing.

I myself am a 4/4 wounded soldier. I have a wounded skull, and three spine joints were damaged. Seventy-five percent of my stomach was cut out. My liver, my spleen, kidney, and bladder were disabled and damaged because of the AO effects. Especially my second child Nguyen Minh Phu. He now is fourteen and studying in the sixth class level. He studies hard and well. But I am worried that he often has headaches, is dazzled. He sleeps all day. He has carbuncles everywhere in his body, especially on his feet and arms.

We are very poor. My wife is weak, but she has to nourish her sick husband, disabled children. So we can't live normally and the children can't go to school. We have invited to Hanoi by the newspaper television station vTV5 to be on the "Family Maker" program. The children were taken care of by the government and leaders of organizations. Phu has attended the general congress of the Vietnam Red Cross, and AO Victims Fund.

My family writes to you respectfully, my Director. Please compose a call to all humans for help. Our family needs your help very much.

Minh Phu's father
Nguyen Quynh Loc
Tam Hop Village,
Tho Thanh, Yen Thanh,
Nghe An Province

■■■

One afternoon, Ken Herrmann visits a small home outside of Danang. Accompanied by Miss Hien, the chief of section social worker for the Danang Red Cross Chapter, and My Hoa, program administrator for the SUNY Brockport Study Abroad Program, he meets Nguyen Giao, the thirty-nine-year-old father of three girls, aged twenty, seventeen, and ten. Mr. Giao is lying upon a mat, unable to walk. His entire body is covered with tumors the size of golf balls. Large soccer ball sized tumors hang from his legs and chest. His skeletal arms and legs are bowed.

When Mr. Giao was a child, his family lived less than one mile from a military base in Danang. Helicopters sprayed the area with something that killed all the fish. One day he ate potatoes that had been doused with Agent Orange. Before long, small tumors started growing on his torso, and within months or a few years, his friends had started to die. In 1980, tumors sprouted like massive mushrooms from his body, leaving him in constant pain, with terrible headaches and fevers. He'd been bedridden for the past ten years.

Sometimes his wife buys painkillers to try to give Nguyen some relief from his pain, but the $3.04 he receives from the government doesn't stretch very far. The family's neighbors help them a little, and Mr. Giao's wife grows rice and vegetables, cleans houses, and washes clothes to add to the family income. She worries about her husband and children.

"He doesn't eat much now. He often just lets his food sit in a bowl on the floor, but he can still feed himself if he wants to," she tells her visitors.

Nguyen's daughters have also developed small tumors, and they suffer from fevers, headaches, dizziness, and vision problems. No one else in this family has ever had these kinds of conditions.

"It all began with my eating a potato and drinking water that had been sprayed."

Asked what he would like to say to the Americans who caused his family's illnesses, he pauses for a very long moment. Nguyen stares intensely at Herrmann.

"I don't blame Americans. I think it is my fate. If they can help my daughters I hope they will."

Miss Hien tells Herrmann that before they were exposed to Agent Orange, this family and thousands of others had no history of these strange illnesses. They've all been tested for exposure to dioxin, and tests indicate that they have been. They all lived in areas that were heavily sprayed with Agent Orange.

Herrmann opens another beer, removes his glasses, and watches great dark clouds roll in from Lake Erie.

"The numbers of victims and the severity of their symptoms are staggering," he says. "One family's grandfather was VC and was sprayed. His son was born with tumors. His grandson was born with tumors. It is obvious that this legacy will haunt Vietnam for generations. One wonders why it does not haunt the conscience of America."

When Ken Herrmann boarded a "freedom bird" in 1969, he swore that he would never return to Vietnam. Certain that the plane wouldn't be shot down, he cheered with other young men, now veterans, and settled in for a dinner of airplane food steak.

"We were safe. We were going home. We had survived the hell known as the Vietnam War. Over time, I realized it was not the nation I had fled at all. It was the war. I had never left the nation at all. It had stayed with me."

Professor Herrmann's staff and the students he asked to help out could not keep up with the avalanche of letters from all over Vietnam. If only these letters could be read on the floor of the US House of Representatives, to members of the British Parliament, to the French Assembly, to people throughout the world who would, if they just knew the circumstances, be willing to help victims of Agent Orange.

Ken Herrmann is not the type to tell war stories. Ask him a question and he will answer, directly, not at all concerned whether you might appreciate his answer. Until I asked about his own exposure to Agent Orange, he didn't mention the endless fixed-wing and helicopter spray missions over the Que Son and Hiep Duc valleys.

"Yeah, they sprayed the valleys and they sprayed us. I had two heart attacks in the 1980s and 1990s, and suffer from ischemia, a heart disease, a recent addition to the VA's list of related Agent Orange disorders. I filed a claim last week, and expect the VA to approve it whenever they get around to doing that."

After more than twenty-five years of waiting, American veterans are being compensated for a wide variety of illnesses related to their exposure to Agent Orange. This only happened because young soldiers who went off to the killing fields of Southeast Asia refused, years later, to give up trying to tell the world what Agent Orange/dioxin does to human beings. Vietnam veterans would not allow the government they served to ridicule their complaints as symptoms of drug abuse, alcoholism, or combat stress.

Year after year, decade after decade, these veterans, their families, and their supporters attended meetings, started organizations, conducted research, created websites, wrote letters, and testified at local and national hearings, demanding that their government stop treating them as throwaway soldiers. There are no records of how many veterans have died premature, painful deaths, their cries for help drowned out by a chorus of stonewalling, denial, political chicanery, and scientific deceit. It's impossible to know how many children have died in their mothers' wombs or shortly after birth from monstrous birth defects. There were no ceremonies to honor these Agent Orange children. Grieving parents were not invited to the White House, nor were they asked to share their stories on national television and radio programs. Fathers and mothers laid their children to rest in lonely cemeteries, knowing these small caskets held victims of chemical warfare.

It appears that at long last our nation has stopped blaming and trying to punish its own veterans for the catastrophe in

Vietnam. Sadly, that is not the case when it comes to Vietnamese victims of the defoliation campaign. The fear of communism and the political expediency and hubris that drove the United States to wage scorched earth warfare in Vietnam have not given way to compassion for the survivors of that terrible destruction.

In many ways, controversy over Agent Orange is like a mass murder case in which the presiding judge refuses to *see* the victims, even though he allows them to appear in court. Those who wish to hold the perpetrator(s) accountable are allowed to speak, even though their testimony will not influence the court's decision. Asked to consider this most peculiar situation, the Supreme Court demurs. Why bother to hear arguments in a case when it's already been established, time and again, that there are no *verifiable* victims?

Scientists from many parts of the world have gone to Vietnam to ascertain the effects of Agent Orange on the Vietnamese people. Their findings indicate that dioxin poses a danger not only to those who were exposed to Agent Orange during and after the war, but quite possibly to future generations of Vietnamese children.

Those who still doubt that our world is inundated with toxic chemicals and that these chemicals lodge in our bodies—undermining our immune systems, destroying our health, and killing our friends and families—might want to pay a visit to Vietnam. There, community workers, doctors, nurses, ex-soldiers, scientists, and others do not just talk about the dangers of carcinogenic, fetus deforming, and mutagenic chemicals; they *show* visitors what Agent Orange/dioxin has done, and is doing, to millions of human beings.

Vietnam is the toxic mirror into which avaricious corporations do not want ordinary people throughout the world to look. Inside of this mirror, we see polluted rivers and streams, dying lakes, poisoned oceans, and contaminated food and water. Inside of this mirror, we discover studies warning us that:

> At present, one-third of all Americans will develop cancer over a lifetime and one in four Americans are likely to die from cancer. . . . The proximate source of almost all dioxin intake in the general population is from food. Using our data for daily dietary dioxin exposure and the EPA's proposed risk specific does, we estimate that over a lifetime a maximum of 30 to 300 excess cancers per million could result from the ingestion of dioxin-containing food products.[1]

Inside of this mirror we find studies with titles like, "More Kids are Getting Brain Cancer. Why?"

> But evidence suggests the rise in these childhood cancers, as well as in cancers like non-Hodgkins' lymphoma and multiple myeloma among adults, may also be partially explained by exposure to chemicals in the environment. . . . Recent epidemiologic studies have shown that as children's exposures to home and garden pesticides increase, so does their risk of non-Hodgkin's lymphoma, brain cancer, and leukemia. Yet right now, you can go to your hardware store and buy lawn pesticides, pain thinner and weed killers, all containing toxic chemicals linked to these diseases.
>
> In both children and adults, the incidence rate for non-Hodgkin's lymphoma has increased thirty percent since 1950. The disease has been linked to industrial

chemicals, chemicals found in agricultural, home, and garden pesticides, as well as dark hair dyes.[2]

It's easy to understand why we are reluctant to look into a mirror that displays the faces of our loved ones, friends, neighbors and colleagues who've died from cancer and other diseases linked to toxic chemicals like dioxin. We want to believe that no sane person would deliberately poison their own children's air, water, and food supplies. Yes, something terrible might have happened in Vietnam; however, that was an accident. That was war. In the United States, the Food and Drug Administration, the Environmental Protection Agency, and state and local laws protect citizens from a domestic form of chemical warfare.

Skeptics, doubters, those who believe the Agent Orange tragedy is a communist conspiracy, and even representatives from corporations that profit from pain and suffering are invited to visit Friendship Village in Hanoi, the Peace Villages in Danang, and the children's ward in Ho Chi Minh City's Tu Du Hospital. The Vietnamese offer visitors bottled water, green tea, biscuits, and fresh fruit. They answer questions in a calm, polite, friendly manner, and they will take you on a tour of the legacies of chemical warfare. There's no reason to fear the Vietnamese people. They will tell you about the toxic holocaust that befell their nation, then allow you to decide whether or not this tragedy happened.

For decades, the United States government appeared to be waiting for Vietnam veterans to die. Now, the chemical companies and the government are waiting for the Vietnamese to give up their campaign to secure justice for the victims of chemical warfare. This will never happen. We ignore their suffering at our own peril.

Selection from "Agent Orange" Product Liability Litigation: Memorandum, Order and Judgment

LEGAL BASIS FOR CLAIMS

a. Alien Tort Statute ("ATS"), US Code U.S.C. Title 28, § 1350;

b. Torture Victim Protection Act ("TVPA"), 28 U.S.C. § 1350 note;

c. War Crimes Act, USC Title 18, § 2441 Geneva Protocol for the Prohibition of the Use in War of Asphyxiating, Poisonous or Other Gases, and of Bacteriological Methods of Warfare, 1925 Annex to the Hague Convention IV, Article 23, Respecting the Laws and Customs of War on Land, signed October 18, 1907;

d. 1925 Geneva Protocol for the Prohibition of the Use in War of Asphyxiating, Poisonous or Other Gases, and of Biological Methods of Warfare;

e. Article 23 of the Annex to the Hague Convention IV, Respecting the Laws and Customs of War on Land, signed October 18, 1907;

f. Geneva Convention relative to Protection of Civilian Persons in Time of War, signed at Geneva on August 12, 1949;

g. Agreement for the Prosecution and Punishment of the Major War Criminals of the European Axis and Charter of the International Military Tribunal at Nuremberg, signed and entered into force on August 8, 1945;

h. United Nations Charter, signed at San Francisco on June 26, 1945 and entered into force on October 24, 1945;

i. United Nations General Assembly Resolution No. 2603-A (1969);

j. Customary international law;

k. Common law of the United States of America;

l. Laws of Vietnam;

m. Common law of the State of New York, including but not limited to product liability, assault and battery, negligence, recklessness, intentional infliction of emotional distress, negligent infliction of emotional distress, civil conspiracy, unjust enrichment and public nuisance.

Class certification is sought. In view of the dismissal of all individual claims, there is no reason to consider the motion for class certification.

THEORIES

a. War Crimes

It is contended that the acts of defendants adversely affecting plaintiffs constitute violations of the laws and customs of war, also known as war crimes, which prohibit: the employment of poison or poisoned weapons or other weapons calculated to cause superfluous injury or unnecessary suffering, the wanton destruction of cities, towns, villages or the national environment, or devastation not justified by military necessity; the use of biological or chemical agents of warfare, whether gaseous, liquid, or solid, employed because of their direct toxic effects on people, animals, or plants; and the poisoning of food and water supplies in the course of war. Leaders, organizers, facilitators, conspirators, and accomplices participating in the formulation and execution of these acts are claimed to be responsible for all acts performed by any person in the execution of this plan. The acts described allegedly constitute war crimes in violation of the ATS, TVPA, customary international law, the common law of the United States, the common law of the State of New York, the laws of Vietnam, and international treaties, agreements, conventions and resolutions.

b. Genocide

It is contended that the acts against plaintiffs constitute genocide, in violation of customary international law which prohibits the following acts committed with intent to destroy, in whole or in part, a national ethnic, racial or religious group, as such: killing members of the group; causing serious bodily or mental harm to members of the group; deliberately inflicting on the group conditions of life calculated to bring about its physical destruction in whole or in part; or imposing measures intended to prevent births within the group. Leaders, organizers, facilitators, conspirators and accomplices participating in the formulation and execution of these acts are claimed to be responsible for all acts performed by any person in execution of such plan.

c. Crimes Against Humanity

It is contended that the acts against plaintiffs constitute crimes against humanity in violation of customary international law, which prohibits inhumane acts of a very serious nature such as willful killing and torture and other inhumane acts committed as part of a widespread or systematic attack against any civilian population or persecutions on political, racial or religious grounds. Leaders, organizers, facilitators, conspirators and accomplices participating in the formulation and execution of these acts are responsible for all acts performed by any person in execution of such plan.

d. Torture.

e. Assault and Battery.

f. International Infliction of Emotional Distress.

g. Negligent Infliction of Emotional Distress.

Defendants, it is claimed, carelessly and negligently inflicted emotional distress through wanton and reckless conduct in manufacturing and supplying herbicides contaminated with dioxin for use in herbicidal warfare. As a direct result of defendants' wrong acts, it is contended, plaintiffs and plaintiffs' immediate family members have suffered and will continue to suffer significant physical injury, pain and suffering and extreme and severe mental anguish and emotional distress. This conduct allegedly constituted the negligent infliction of emotional distress.

h. Strict Product Liability

The negligence of the defendants, their servants, employees

and agents consisted, according to the complaint, in manufacturing and supplying the herbicides without making proper
and sufficient tests to determine their dangers and contraindications, in that defendants knew, or in the exercise of
reasonable diligence, should have known that the herbicides
were unsafe and unfit for use by reason of the dangerous effects
to human health and the environment, in negligently failing to
adequately warn the public and the United States and RVN
governments of the dangers and contraindications of the herbicides, in failing to properly inspect the herbicides, and in
concealing the dangers and contraindications of the herbicides
from the public and from the United States and RVN governments in order to profit from the manufacture and supply
of the herbicides. It is contended that defendants are liable
jointly and severally to the plaintiffs under the doctrine of
strict product liability.

Vietnamese Studies on Agent Orange/Dioxin

Ba Thinh, Hoang. *A Hero of the Armed Forces who Met Uncle Ho Three Times and His Children and Grandchildren Affected by Agent Orange/Dioxin.* Hanoi: Research Centre on Gender, Family and Environment in Development (CGFED), 2005.

———. "A Family with Three Generations Affected by Agent Orange/Dioxin." Hanoi: CGFED, 2003.

Din Cau, Hoang. *Environment and Health in Vietnam (30 years after the Operation Ranch Hand),* Hanoi: Nghe An Publishing House, Centre on Studies and Dissemination of Encyclopedic Knowledge, 2003.

Dai, Le Can. *Agent Orange in the War in Vietnam—Situation and Consequences.* Hanoi: Red Cross, 1999.

Minh, Tu Binh, et al. "Chapter 11 Persistent Organic Pollutants in Vietnam: Levels, Patterns, Trends, and Human Health Implications." *Developments in Environmental Sciences* 7 (2007): 515–555.

Ministry of Health. *Summary Report of the Vietnam-US Symposium on the Impacts of Agent Orange/Dioxin on Human Health and Environment.* Hanoi, 2002.

Ministry of Labour, Invalid and Social Affairs. *Analysis of Children with Disabilities in Vietnam.* Hanoi: UNICEF, 2004.

Sajor, Indai and Le Thi Nham Tuyet. "Agent Orange: Impact of Chemical Warfare on the Reproductive Rights of Women and Men in Vietnam." Hanoi: CGFED, 2000.

Tlhi Xinh, Phan, et al. "Unique Secondary Chromosomal Abnormalities are Frequently Found in the Chronic Phase of Chronic Myeloid Leukemia in Southern Vietnam." *Cancer Genetics and Cytogenetics* 168, no. 1 (July 2006): 59–68.

Tuan, Anh Mai, et al. "Dioxin Contamination in Soils of Southern Vietnam." *Chemosphere* 67, no. 9 (April 2007): 1802–1807.

Tuyet, Le Thi Nham and Annika Johansson. "Impact of Chemical Warfare with Agent Orange on Women's Reproductive Lives in Vietnam: A Pilot Study." *Reproductive Health Matters* 9, no. 18 (November 2001): 156–164.

Tuyet, Le Thi Nham and Pham Huong Thao. *Case Study of Mr. Nguyen Dinh Hanh, Bien Hoa City, Dong Nai Province.* Hanoi: CGFED, 2005.

MORE SCIENTIFIC STUDIES

Bajgar, Jiri et al. "Global Impact of Chemical Warfare Agents Used Before and After 1945." *Handbook of Toxicology of Chemical Warfare Agents*, 2009, 17–24.

Dwernchuk, Wayne L. et. al. "Dioxin Reservoirs in Southern Vietnam—A Legacy of Agent Orange." *Chemosphere* 47, no.2 (April 2002): 117–137.

Ginevan, Michael E. et al. "Assessing Exposure to Allied

Ground Troops in the Vietnam War: A Quantitative Evaluation of the Stellman Exposure Opportunity Index Model." *Chemosphere* 75, no. 11 (June 2009): 1512–1518.

Hall, Wayne. "The Logic of Controversy: The Case of Agent Orange in Australia." *Social Science & Medicine* 29, no. 4 (1989): 537–544.

Kalter, Harold. "Teratology in the 20th Century Environmental Causes of Congenital Malformations in Humans and How They Were Established." *Teratology in the Twentieth Century*, Elsevier, 2003: 131–282.

Mortelmans, Kristien et al. "Mutagenicity of Agent Orange Components and Related Chemicals." *Toxicology and Applied Pharmacology* 75, no. 1 (August 1984): 137–146.

Palmer, Michael G. "The Legacy of Agent Orange: Empirical Evidence from Central Vietnam." *Social Science & Medicine* 60, no. 5 (March 2005): 1061–1070.

Schecter, Arnold et al. "Dioxins: An Overview," *Environmental Research* 101, no. 3 (July 2006): 419–428.

———. "Chlorinatead Dioxin, Dbenzofuran, Coplanar, Mono-ortho, and Di-ortho Substituted PCB Cogener Levels in Blood and Semen of Michigan Vietnam Veterans Compared with Levels in Vietnamese Exposed to Agent Orange." *Chemosphere* 27 (1993): 241–252.

———. "Dioxin and Dibenzofuran Levels in Blood and Adipose Tissue of Vietnamese from Various Locations in Vietnam in Proximity to Agent Orange Spraying." *Chemosphere* 25 (1992).

———. "Human Adipose Tissue Dioxin and Dibenzofuran Levels and 'Dioxin Toxic Equivalents' in Patients from the North and South of Vietnam." *Chemosphere* 20, no. 7–9 (1990): 943–950.

———. "Elevated Body Burdens of 2,3,7,8-tetrachlorodibenzodioxin in Adipose Tissue of United States Vietnam Veterans." *Chemosphere* 18 (1989): 431–438.

———. "Adipose Tissue Levels of 2,3,7,8 TCDD in Vietnamese Adults Living in Vietnam, 1984–1987." *Chemosphere*, 18 (1989): 1057–1062.

———. "Levels of 2,3,7,8-TCDD in Silt Samples Collected Between 1985–1986 from Rivers in the North and South of Vietnam." *Chemosphere* 19, no. 1–6 (1986): 547–550.

Verger, P., et al. "Correlation Between Dioxin Levels in Adipose Tissue and Estimated Exposure to Agent Orange in South Vietnamese Residents." *Research* 65, no. 2 (May 1994): 226–242.

VA: Veterans' Diseases Associated with Agent Orange Exposure

Acute and Subacute Transient Peripheral Neuropathy
A nervous system condition that causes numbness, tingling, and motor weakness. Under the VA's rating regulations, it must be at least ten percent disabling within one year of exposure to Agent Orange and must resolve within two years after the date it began.

AL Amyloidosis
A rare disease caused when an abnormal protein, amyloid, enters tissues or organs.

B Cell Leukemias
Cancers which affect B cells, such as hairy cell leukemia.

Chloracne

A skin condition that occurs soon after dioxin exposure and that looks like common forms of acne seen in teenagers. Under the VA's rating regulations, it must be at least ten percent disabling within one year of exposure to Agent Orange.

Chronic Lymphocytic Leukemia

A disease that progresses slowly with increasing production of excessive numbers of white blood cells.

Diabetes Mellitus (Type 2)

A disease characterized by high blood sugar levels, resulting from the body's inability to respond properly to the hormone insulin.

Hodgkin's Disease

A malignant lymphoma (cancer) characterized by progressive enlargement of the lymph nodes, liver, and spleen, as well as by progressive anemia.

Ischemic Heart Disease

A disease characterized by a reduced supply of blood to the heart.

Multiple Myeloma

A cancer of specific bone marrow cells that is characterized by bone marrow tumors in various bones of the body.

Parkinson's Disease

A motor system condition with symptoms that include trembling of the limbs and face and impaired balance.

Porphyria Cutanea Tarda
A disorder characterized by liver dysfunction and by thinning and blistering of the skin in sun-exposed areas. Under the VA's rating regulations, it must be at least ten percent disabling within one year of exposure to Agent Orange.

Prostate Cancer
Cancer of the prostate, one of the most common cancers among men.

Soft Tissue Sarcoma (other than Osteosarcoma, Chondrosarcoma, Kaposi's sarcoma, or Mesothelioma)
A group of different types of cancers in body tissues such as muscle, fat, blood, lymph vessels, and connective tissues.*

* Source: United States Department of Veterans Affairs, 2009.

Agent Orange: Important Dates

1940s. Arthur W. Galston, a graduate student at the University of Illinois, discovers that chemicals that inhibit plant growth can also increase the number of floral buds and harvestable pods produced on soybean plants getting ready to flower. Scientific studies on the effects of growth inhibiters continue during World War II at Ft. Detrick, Maryland.

1950. President Dwight Eisenhower refuses to sign an order that would allow the use of herbicides in Korea.

1950s. Research on herbicides continues at Ft. Detrick, Maryland.

1959. The United States military experiments with herbicides at Fort Drum, New York.

1961. President John F. Kennedy approves of using herbicides in Vietnam. Tests of herbicides on the Vietnamese countryside begin in August 1961, and continue through December.

1962. The first shipment of Agent Orange arrives in Vietnam. Systematic testing continues for years.

1965. Operation Ranch Hand, "Only we can prevent forests," uses Agent Orange in Vietnam.

1966. Professor Arthur W. Galston and twelve colleagues from the American Society of Plant Physiologists send a letter to President Lyndon B. Johnson expressing their concerns that herbicides might harm human beings in Vietnam, and challenging the use of herbicides to destroy food crops.

1967. A team of Japanese filmmakers talk with Vietnamese who live in areas where Agent Orange has been used.

1969. Dr. Bert Pfeiffer and other scientists from the Council of the American Association for the Advancement of Science pass a resolution urging the Department of Defense to "immediately cease all use of 2,4-D and 2,4,5-T in Vietnam."

1969. Bionetics Laboratories of Bethesda, Maryland, releases the results of its study, completed in 1965, which demonstrates that even in the lowest dose given, 2,4-5-T causes cleft palates, missing and deformed eyes, cystic kidneys, and enlarged livers in the offspring of laboratory animals.

1970. Congress directs the Department of Defense to engage the National Academy of Sciences to conduct a comprehensive study of the ecological and physiological effects of Agent Orange in Vietnam.

1970. On April 15, 1970, Deputy Secretary of Defense David

Packard announces the immediate suspension of the use of 2,4,5-T in Vietnam. Also, the Surgeon General reports to the Hart committee on the restrictions placed on 2,4,5-T: suspension of liquid formulation for home use, suspension of all aquatic uses, intent to cancel registration of nonliquid formulations for use around homes and on all food crops.

1970. Thomas Whiteside writes in the June 20, 1970, issue of the *New Yorker* that the sale and use of 2,4,5-T continues within the United States.

1978. Paul Rheutershan announces that he "died in Vietnam and didn't even know it." Beginning of class action lawsuit on behalf of Vietnam veterans and their families.

1979. Environmental Protection Agency issues emergency suspension of 2,4,5-T and 2,4,5-TP (Silvex) in the United States.

1984. Vietnam veterans' class action lawsuit is settled out of court for $180 million.

1984. "Fairness Hearings" into out-of-court settlement begin in Brooklyn Federal Court.

1990. Admiral Elmo Zumwalt Jr. completes a classified study for the Department of Veterans Affairs.

1991. The Agent Orange Act directs the Secretary of Veterans Affairs to request the National Academy of Sciences to conduct a comprehensive study of scientific studies and medical information on the health effects of exposure to herbicides in

Vietnam. The Academy will include in their study the possible effects of dioxin on human beings.

1994. Wayne Dwernychuk, a scientist working with Hatfield Consultants, meets with Committee 33 in Vietnam.

2004. Lawyers acting on behalf of Vietnamese victims of Agent Orange launch a class action suit charging Dow Chemical, et al. with war crimes.

2005. Judge Jack B. Weinstein dismisses the Vietnamese lawsuit. Lawyers file an appeal.

2007. A court of appeals rules against Vietnamese plaintiffs' attempt to reinstate their class action lawsuit.

Acknowlegments

I would like to thank the following people for their love and support of victims of chemical warfare, for their support of and belief in this book, and for their excellent advice and professional editing:

Dr. Professor Nguyen Trong Nhan, Dr. Nguyen Thi Ngoc Phuong, Nguyen Thi Hien, Nguyen Thi My Hoa, Chairman Nguyen Dinh An, Nguyen Thi Nga, Dr. Pham VietThan, Professor Phung Tuu Boi, Nguyen Mai Phuc Minh , Dr. Wayne Dwernychuk, Professor John Marciano, Dr. Michael Viola, Paul Sutton, Howard Zinn, Noam Chomsky, Jeff Cohen, Jack Hopper, Maura Stephens, George Sapio, Adelaide Gomer, Kenneth J. Herrmann, Richard Hughes, Dean Kokkoris, Trinh Kokkoris, Rev. Peter Phan Khac Tu, Gabe Espinal, Elizabeth DeLong, Dan Simon, Ruth Weiner, Beverly Cherweznik, Joyce Garwood, Marian MacCurdy, Sandi Strait, Jerry Strait Sandra Steingrabber, Elizabeth McAlister, Phoebe Wilcox, Gilea Hurley, Danica Wilcox, and Brendan Wilcox.

Notes

INTRODUCTION

No notes.

CHAPTER 1: ECOCIDE

1. Memorandum from Secretary of State Rusk to President Kennedy, November 24, 1961. Quoted in "Memorandum of Law in Support of Defendants' Motion to Dismiss All Claims in Plaintiffs' Amended Class Action Complaint for Lack of Jurisdiction over the Subject Matter and for Failure to State a Claim upon Which Relief Can Be Granted." U.S. District of New York, 2005: 9.
2. Constantine P. Kokkoris, Amended Complaint in The Vietnam Association for Vietnam Victims of Agent Orange/Dioxin, et al., v. The Dow Chemical Co., U.S. District Court for the Eastern District of New York, docket No. 04CV 0400: 14.
3. Ibid., 17.
4. Ibid., 15.
5. Ibid., 18.
6. Ibid., 15.
7. "Memorandum of Law," 11–12.
8. Barry Weisberg, *The Ecology of War* (San Francisco: Canfield Press, 1970) 18–19.
9. Ibid., 4.
10. Secret Confidential Report, *Operation Pink Rose*, 1967. Declassified and Regraded, By order of the Secretary of the Army, 1988, 3.
11. Allied Leaflet, AH 23365.
12. *Operation Pink Rose.*
13. Ibid.
14. Ibid.
15. Ibid.
16. Ibid.
17. Weisberg, *The Ecology of War*, 69.
18. Tom Mangold and John Penycate, *The Tunnels of Cu Chi* (New York: Ballantine Books, 2005.)
19. Arthur H. Westing, "Chemical Warfare Against Vegetation in Vietnam," *Environmental Awareness* 25, no. 2 (2002), 51–58.

20. Vo Guy, "The Attack of Agent Orange on the Environment in Vietnam and its Consequences," presented at International Conference on Agent Orange/Dioxin, Paris, 2005.

21. Ibid.

22. Westing, "Return to Vietnam: the Legacy of Agent Orange," lecture, Yale University, 2002.

23. "Statement on the Geneva Protocol of 1925 and the Biological Weapons Convention January 22, 1975." *The American Presidency Project*. http://www.presidency.ucsb.edu/ws/index.php?pid=5049&st=Geneva+Protocol&st1=#axzz1HiN7DpbE.

24. Thomas Whiteside, *Defoliation* (New York: Ballantine, 1970), 74.

25. Ibid., 99.

CHAPTER 2: TRANSFORMATIONS

1. Fred A. Wilcox, *Waiting for an Army to Die: The Tragedy of Agent Orange* (New York: Random House, 1983), 51–53.

2. Ibid.

3. Ibid.

4. Michelle Mason, *The Friendship Village* (Cypress Park Productions, 2002), DVD.

5. Ibid.

6. "Nation: Where is My Country?" *Time*, February 25, 1980, http://www.time.com/time/magazine/article/0,9171,952592,00.html.

7. Louis Edwards, "Genetic Damage in New Zealand Vietnam War Veterans," Institute of Molecular Biosciences (Massey University, 2006), 12.

8. Ibid.

9. Ibid.

10. "Johnny can't read, sit still, or stop hitting the neighbor's kid. Why?" 7 vols. Mount Sinai School of Medicine, Center for Children's Health and the Environment, no date.

11. Ibid.

CHAPTER 3: PROMISES

1. Dr. Professor Nguyen Nhan, "The Chemical Warfare and Its Consequences in Vietnam" *Proceedings of The International Conference of Victims of Agent Orange/Dioxin*, March 28–29, 2006, 11.

2. Ibid., 12–13.

3. Nhan, "To The American People: An Open Letter," Hanoi: Vietnam Association For Victims of Agent Orange/Dioxin, August 6, 2004.

4. Le Thi, *Anthropology Review*, January 1, 2006, 49–50.

5. Ibid.

6. Ibid.

7. Ibid.

8. Nhan, "To the American People," 2004.

9. Ibid.

10. Ibid.

11. Ibid.
12. Nhan, "Agent Orange and the Conscience of the USA," presented at annual conference of the American Studies Association in Albuquerque, October 2008.
13. Ibid.
14. Ibid.
15. Admiral E. R. Zumwalt Jr., "Report to Secretary of the Department of Veterans Affairs on the Association between Adverse Health Effects and Exposure to Agent Orange," May 5, 1990, 36.
16. Ibid., 33.
17. Ibid., 33.
18. Ibid., 33.
19. Ibid., 35.
20. Ibid., 22.
21. Ibid., 50–51.
22. Nhan, "Agent Orange and the Conscience of the USA," 2008.
23. Sandra C. Taylor, *Vietnamese Women at War* (University Press of Kansas, 1999), 33.
24. Gerson Smoger, Interview with *Thanh Nien News*, no date.
25. Huu Ngoc Ngoc, *Wandering Through Vietnamese Culture* (Hanoi: The Gioi Publishers, 1995), 6.

CHAPTER 4: SPRAYED AND BETRAYED

1. Fred A. Wilcox, *Waiting for an Army to Die: The Tragedy of Agent Orange*, (New York: Seven Stories Press 2011), 100.
2. Ibid., 100.
3. Ibid., 101.
4. Ibid., 102.
5. Ibid., 105.
6. Ibid., 105.
7. Ibid., 105.
8. Ibid., 106.
9. Ibid., 106.
10. Courtroom testimony, Fairness Hearings, Brooklyn Federal Court, June 1985.
11. Ibid.
12. Ibid.
13. Wilcox, "Waiting for an Army to Die," xvi

CHAPTER 5: A LUCKY MAN

No notes.

CHAPTER 6: GENERATIONS

No notes.

CHAPTER 7: JURISPRUDENCE

1. Vietnam Association v. Dow Chemical, United States District Court, Eastern District of New York, March 18, 2004, 23.
2. The Commonwealth of Massachusetts, *Mortality among Vietnam Veterans in Massachusetts, 1972–1983*, Report for the Veterans Administration, Washington, DC.
3. Barclay M. Shepard, et al., *Proportionate Mortality Study of Army and Marine Corps Veterans of the Vietnam War*, Office of Environmental Epidemiology, Veterans Administration, 1987.
4. L. P. H. Anderson et al., *Wisconsin Vietnam Veteran Mortality Study*, Madison, WI, Division of Health, 1985.
5. A. P. Holmes, *West Virginia Vietnam-Era Veterans Mortality Study*, Charleston, West Virginia Health Department, no date.
6. M. J. Fett et al., *Australian Veterans Health Studies: The Mortality Report* (Canberra: Australian Government Publishing Service, 1984.)
7. Ed Kozel, *Agent Orange Primer* (No publisher given, 2009), 23.
8. Constantine P. Korkkoris, Amended Class Action Complaint, MDL 381, 48.
9. Michael Palmer, Project *MUSE, Scholarly Journal Online*, 176.
10. L. W. Dwernychuk, et al., "Dioxin Reservoirs in Southern Vietnam: A Legacy of Agent Orange," *Chemosphere* 47 (2002): 117–137.
11. Korkkoris, "Complaint," 49.
12. Jack B. Weinstein, "Agent Orange Product Liability Litigation: Memorandum, Order, and Judgment." MDL No. 381, 04-CV-400, 42.
13. Unclassified cable from US ambassador in Vietnam to Secretary of State, Washington, DC, February 16, 2003.
14. Kenn Hermann, "Agent Orange research canceled: 'A series of lies, deceit and blackmail,'" *Political Affairs Magazine,* April 2005.
15. Weinstein, "Memorandum," 43.
16. Ibid., 43–44.
17. Ibid., 45.
18. Fred A. Wilcox, *Waiting for an Army to Die: The Tragedy of Agent Orange* (New York: Seven Stories Press, 2011), 127.
19. Ibid., 128.
20. Ibid., 128.
21. Ibid.
22. Weinstein, "Memorandum," 17.
23. Ibid., 192.
24. Gerson Smoger, interview by *Thanh Nien News,* no date.
25. Wilcox, *Uncommon Martyrs,* (New York: Addison-Wesley, 1991), 95–96.
26. Weinstein, "Memorandum," 155.
27. Weinstein, "Memorandum," 182–4.
28. Ibid., 183.
29. Ibid., 178.
30. Ibid., 178.
31. Ibid., 181–2.

32. "Memorandum of Law in Support of Defendants' Motion to Dismiss All Claims in Plaintiffs' Amended Class Action Complaint for Lack of Jurisdiction over the Subject Matter and for Failure to State a Claim upon Which Relief Can Be Granted," US District of New York, 2005, 6–19.

CHAPTER 8: THE LAST FAMILY

1. Dr. Professor Tran Xuan Thu, "Comments From the Scientists on the Consequences of Chemical Warfare in Vietnam," Proceedings, The International Conference of Victims of Agent Orange, Hanoi, March 28–29, 2006, 18–19.
2. Fred A. Wilcox, *Waiting for an Army to Die: The Tragedy of Agent Orange*, (New York: Seven Stories Press, 2011), 53.
3. Ibid., 53.
4. Ibid., 54.
5. Louise Edwards, "Genetic Damage in New Zealand Vietnam War Veterans," Institute of Molecular Biosciences, Massey University, 2006, 15.
6. Ibid., 1.

CHAPTER 9: THE REALM

1. *The Militant*, July 9, 2007.
2. Transcript of Preliminary Hearing Before The Honorable Jack B. Weinstein, United States District Judge, Vietnamese Class Action Suit, United States District Court, March 18, 2004, 16–19.
3. Ibid., 24.
4. Jack B. Weinstein, Agent Orange Product Liability Litigation: Memorandum, Order, and Judgment, MDL No. 381, O4-CV-400, 44.
5. Wayne Dwernychuk, Interview with *Thahn Nien News*, August 8, 2009.
6. "Memorandum of Law in Support of Defendants' Motion to Dismiss All Claims in Plaintiffs' Amended Class Action Complaint for Lack of Jurisdiction over the Subject Matter and for Failure to State a Claim upon Which Relief Can Be Granted," US District of New York, 2005, 62.
7. Weinstein, "Memorandum," 156–165.

CHAPTER 10: FREE FIRE ZONE

1. Tom Mangold and John Penycate, *The Tunnels of Chu Chi* (New York: Ballantine, 1985.)
2. Ibid.
3. Stanley Karnow, *Vietnam: A History* (New York: Penguin, 1983), 213.
4. Fred A. Wilcox, *Waiting for an Army to Die: The Tragedy of Agent Orange* (New York: Seven Stories Press, 2011), 172.
5. Ngo D. Anh et al., "Association between Agent Orange and birth defects: Systematic Review and meta-analysis," *International Journal of Epidemiology* 35 (2006): 1220–1230.
6. Ibid., 1227.

7. Wilcox, *Waiting for an Army to Die*, 55.
8. Ibid.

CHAPTER 11: CHEMICAL CHILDREN

1. *Cheer Up, Viet and Duc!* No date.

CHAPTER 12: EVIDENCE ROOM

1. Barry Weisberg, *Ecocide In Indochina*, (San Francisco: Canfield Press, 1970), 59.
2. Ibid., 60.
3. Rachel Carson, *Silent Spring* (New York: Houghton Mifflin, 1962), 29.
4. Thomas Whiteside, *The Withering Rain: America's Herbicidal Folly* (New York: E. P. Dutton, 1971), 13–14.
5. Daniel Shea, "Their Deaths Require Justice and the Living Victims Need To be Compensated and We All Must work to End the Insanity of War," International Conference Of Victims Of Agent Orange/Dioxin, March 28–29, 2006, 62.
6. J. B. Neilands, *Harvest of Death* (New York: Free Press, 1972), 200.

CHAPTER 13: LETTERS DON'T LIE

1. Arnold Schecter and James Olson, "Cancer risk assessment using blood and dioxin levels and daily dietary TEQ intake in general populations of industrial and non-industrial countries," *Chemosphere* 34 (1967): 1569–1577.
2. "More kids are getting brain cancer. Why?" New York: Center for Children's Health and the Environment, Mount Sinai School of Medicine, no date.

Bibliography

An, Le Quy. "Vietnamese Policy on the Environment and Sustainable Development in Environmental Policy and Management in Vietnam." Berlin: German Foundation for International Development, 1997.

Boi, Tuu Boi, et al. "Impact of chemical Warfare (1961–1971) on forest resources of Vietnam." (Presented at the Vietnam-United States Scientific Conference on Human Health and Environmental Effects of Agent Orange/Dioxin, Hanoi, March 3–6, 2002.)

Brown, Michael. *Laying Waste: The Poisoning of America by Toxic Chemicals.* New York: Pantheon, 1980.

Carson, Rachel. *Silent Spring.* New York: Houghton Mifflin, 1962.

Colborn, Theo et. al. *Our Stolen Future.* New York: Plume, 1997.

Committee on the Assessment of Wartime Exposure to Herbicides in Vietnam, Board on Health Promotion and Disease Prevention. *Characterizing Exposure of Veterans to Agent Orange and Other Herbicides Used in Vietnam: Interim Findings and Recommendations.* Institute of Medicine of the National Academies, no date.

Davis, Devra. *The Secret History of the War on Cancer.* New York: Basic Books, 2007.

Dux, John, and P. J. Young. *Agent Orange: The Bitter Harvest.* Sydney: Hodder and Stoughton, 1980.

Dwernychuk, L. W. et al. "Dioxin Reservoirs in Southern Vietnam: A Legacy of Agent Orange." *Chemosphere* 47, no. 2: 117–137.

Dwernychuk, Wayne. "The Extent and Patterns of Usage of Agent Orange and Other Herbicdes in Vietnam Stellman et al." *Nature* 422 (2003): 681–687.

"ECOSYSTEMS: Long-Term Consequences of the Vietnam War." Report to the Environmental Conference on Cambodia, Laos, and Vietnam, Stockholm, Sweden, July 26–28, 2002.

Ensign, Tod, and Michael Uhl. *GI Guinea Pigs: How the Pentagon Exposed Our Troops to Dangers More Deadly Than War.* New York: Playboy Press, 1980.

Epstein, Samuel S. *The Politics of Cancer Revisited.* Fremont Center: East Ridge Press, 1998.

Franco-Vietnamese Friendship Association. *Agent Orange in Vietnam: Yesterday's Crime, Today's Tragedy.* Hanoi: National Political Publishing House, 2008.

Fuller, John G. *The Poison that Fell from the Sky.* New York: Random House, 1977.

Galston, Arthur. *Science and Social Responsibility: A Case History.* New Haven: Yale University, no date.

Hatfield Consultants & 10–80 Committee. *Development of Impact Mitigation Strategies Related to the Use of Agent Orange Herbicide in the Aluoi Valley, Vietnam.* West Vancouver, 2000.

Howard, Michael C., ed. *Asia's Environmental Crisis.* San Francisco: Westview Press, 1993.

Herrmann, Ken. *Lepers and Lunacy: An American in Vietnam Today.* Self published, 2003.

Hersh, Seymour. *Chemical and Biological Warfare: America's Hidden Arsenal.* Indianapolis: Bobbs-Merrill, 1968.

Institute of Anthropology, Vietnamese Academy of Social Sciences. *Special Issue on Victims of Agent Orange/Dioxin in Vietnam.* Hanoi: 2006.

Karnow, Stanley. *Vietnam: A History.* New York: Penguin, 1983.

Linedecker, Clifford Kerr. *Agent Orange and an American Family.* New York: Dell, 1982.

Mangold, Tom and John Penycate. *The Tunnels of Chu Chi.* New York: Ballantine Books, 1985.

Neilnds, J. B. *Harvest of Death: Chemical Warfare In Vietnam and Cambodia.* New York: The Free Press, 1972.

Ngoc, Huu. *Wandering Through Vietnamese Culture.* Hanoi: The Gioi Publishers, 2004.

Schuck, Peter H. *Agent Orange on Trial: Mass Toxic Disasters in the Courts.* Cambridge: Belknap Press, 1987.

Servo, Richard and Milford Lewis. *The Wages of War.* New York: Simon and Schuster, 1990.

Steingraber, Sandra. *Having Faith: An Ecologist's Journey to Motherhood.* New York: The Berkeley Publishing Company, 2003.

———. *Living Downstream.* New York: Vintage, 1998.

"Veterans' Diseases Associated with Agent Orange Exposure." US Department of Veterans Affairs. Updated May 5, 2011. http://www.publichealth.VA.gov/exposures/agentorange/diseases.asp.

Vo Guy. "The Attack of Agent Orange on the Environment in Vietnam and its Consequences." Talk delivered at Paris Conference on Agent Orange/Dioxin, 2005.

———. "The Wound of War: Vietnam Struggles to Erase the Scars of 30 Violent Years." *CERES, The FAO Review* 134 (1992).

Weinstein, Jack B. "Agent Orange Product Liability and Litigation Memorandum, Order and Judgment." MDL No. 381, 04-cv-400.

Westing, Arthur H. "Chemical Warfare Against Vegetation in Vietnam." *Environmental Awareness* 25, no. 2 (2002).

Weisberg, Barry. *Ecocide in Indochina: The Ecology of War.* San Francisco: Canfield Press, 1970.

Wilcox, Fred A. *Waiting for an Army to Die: The Tragedy of Agent Orange.* New York: Seven Stories Press, 2011.

Whiteside, Thomas. *The Pendulum and the Toxic Cloud: The Course of Dioxin Contamination.* New Haven: Yale University Press, 1979.

———. *The Withering Rain: America's Herbicidal Folly.* New York: E.P Dutton, 1971.

———. *Defoliation: What Are Our Herbicides Doing to Us?* New York: Ballantine, 1970.

Zumwalt, Admiral Elmo. Jr. and Lt. Elmo Zumwalt III. *My Father, My Son.* New York: Dell, 1986.

Index

About the Author

Fred A. Wilcox has been a veteran's advocate, environmentalist, and scholar on the Vietnam War for the past thirty years. His book *Waiting for an Army to Die: The Tragedy of Agent Orange* helped break the story of the effects of chemical warfare on US veterans of the Vietnam War when it was first published in 1983. He is the recipient of numerous awards for his scholarship, including the Four Chaplains Humanitarian Award presented to him on two occasions by the Vietnam Veterans of America. He lives in Ithaca, New York, where he is an associate professor of writing at Ithaca College.

About
Seven Stories
Press

Seven Stories Press is an independent book publisher based in New York City. We publish works of the imagination by such writers as Nelson Algren, Russell Banks, Octavia E. Butler, Ani DiFranco, Assia Djebar, Ariel Dorfman, Coco Fusco, Barry Gifford, Hwang Sok-yong, Lee Stringer, and Kurt Vonnegut, to name a few, together with political titles by voices of conscience, including the Boston Women's Health Collective, Noam Chomsky, Angela Y. Davis, Human Rights Watch, Derrick Jensen, Ralph Nader, Loretta Napoleoni, Gary Null, Project Censored, Barbara Seaman, Alice Walker, Gary Webb, and Howard Zinn, among many others. Seven Stories Press believes publishers have a special responsibility to defend free speech and human rights, and to celebrate the gifts of the human imagination, wherever we can. For additional information, visit www.sevenstories.com.